Modern
Libertarianism

Modern Libertarianism

A Brief History of Classical Liberalism
in the United States

Brian Doherty

CATO INSTITUTE
WASHINGTON, DC

Hardcover ISBN: 978-1-964524-42-9
eBook ISBN: 978-1-964524-41-2
Audiobook: 978-1-964524-43-6

Library of Congress Control Number: 2024050129

Printed in the United States of America.

CATO INSTITUTE
1000 Massachusetts Ave. NW
Washington, DC 20001
www.cato.org

For David Boaz,
whose writing and guidance as executive vice president of the
Cato Institute carried on and exemplified the best of the
American libertarian tradition.

C O N T E N T S

Introduction

What is the American libertarian movement? It is a largely unorganized group of intellectuals, economists, journalists, activists, think tankers, politicians, and storytellers striving to change American ideology—and through that American politics. The movement's efforts include well-funded public policy research institutes, political opinion magazines, pro bono litigators, bloggers, novelists, training and funding centers for college professors, and America's most successful, longest-lasting third political party.

Libertarians advocate a simple idea with rich and complicated implications: government, if it has any purpose (many libertarians think it doesn't), should do nothing but protect its citizens' lives and property from direct violence and theft.

Why do libertarians think that? For one, their understanding of economics leads them to believe that a free people would spontaneously develop the institutions that a healthy and wealthy culture needs. Most government attempts to redistribute wealth—or to manage the economy through taxing or regulating—make society poorer without making it any safer or fairer.

The implications of that idea can seem radical indeed: from legalizing all drugs to leaving education, money, and credit to the free market; from financing roads entirely through user fees to bringing overseas troops home; from managing potential harms from new medications through tort law rather than top-down regulation to eliminating antitrust law.

However radical their conclusions, most libertarians believe that the Founding principles of the United States are also their principles. The federal government's original constitutional role was limited to a small set of explicitly delegated powers.

The libertarian movement in America contains many who believe in a government somewhat like one that in theory was established by the US Constitution: a government of limited powers surrounded by a sea of rights both explicit and implicit. But it also contains many anarchists, who often call themselves "anarcho-capitalists" to distinguish themselves from so-called anarchists who don't believe private property is legitimate.

Though rooted in the American Founding, the libertarian vision is not reactionary. It extends into "progressive" areas of sex, drugs, and science—no restrictions on, or unequal state treatment of, stem cell research, cloning, gay marriage, gender identity, cryptography, biotech, or space travel.

Although radical, libertarianism is not utopian. Libertarians believe that economics and human nature impose limits on the degree to which humans can reshape society to achieve grand goals.

We now live in a postcommunist world where the tyranny and poverty created by supposedly benevolent attempts to impose equality are clear, in the aftermath of a 20th century during which governments impoverished, imprisoned, and killed more millions than a sane mind can comprehend.

Meanwhile, since the start of the 20th century, the world has seen enormous increases in human material well-being, life expectancy, and health that occurred largely in lockstep with the spread of market liberalism across the globe and in connection with increasing levels of market freedom. For just some examples, the gross domestic product of the world's economy has increased by more than 40 times since the start of the 20th century (from $3.4 trillion to $121.0 trillion), while global life expectancy has more than doubled in the past two centuries, to more than 72 years. Meanwhile, infant mortality in the United States fell more than 95 percent over the past century—in just the past 30 years, worldwide infant mortality was cut in half. In addition, the rate of battlefield deaths worldwide fell by more than 95 percent in the past 60 years. The percentage of the world's population that was undernourished fell by more than two-thirds over the past 50 years; global cereal yields tripled over the past 60 years; and we are getting more and more value per time spent working and earning worldwide, with Americans specifically now spending less than half their income on basic necessities, compared with 80 percent at the turn of the 20th century.[1]

And humanity isn't achieving these things by despoiling and using up our natural patrimony: the area of the earth covered by trees grew by 2.24 million square kilometers from 1982 to 2016, with Europe's tree canopy growing by 35 percent and that of the United States by 34 percent.[2] And although one would assume the great likelihood of natural resources getting more expensive as they got scarcer, in fact, of 50 major important natural commodities, including metals, energy, and food, the inflation-adjusted price of 43 of them fell from 1982 to 2017, with their real price overall falling by 36.3 percent; translated to the amount of average hourly income required to obtain them, they fell by 64.7 percent.[3]

With such evidence of the wealth-increasing powers unleashed by even small and incremental increases in market freedom, the cause the libertarian movement fought for over the past 70 years seems more and more relevant, even as it is threatened in various ways. We are now in a 21st century when international power politics and medieval religious throwbacks threaten chaos; fiscal doom looms for the 20th century's entitlement state; technology is carving huge arenas of commerce, finance, and communication where calls for government regulation grow louder, yet might be recognized more widely by the citizenry as unnecessary (even as existing regulatory bureaucracies will continue to fight to control those new technologies); and humans could be (as much of a long shot as it seems now) on the cusp of building new societies on the high seas or off the surface of the planet. In this century, the daily papers are filled with stories of new possibilities for production, communication, and commerce—from 3D printing to the "sharing economy"—that promise better lives for most yet which government seems set on delaying or destroying.

The more our powers and wealth increase, the more many see libertarian ideas' relevance as perhaps for that very reason attenuated. We already have the benefits of a restricted free-market capitalism, a common objection goes, so why should we feel compelled to give even more free rein to corporations and entrepreneurs? In the wake of the COVID-19 pandemic that many saw as demanding mass restriction of human working and social behavior allegedly in the name of public health; social and cultural unrest often connected to changes in the distribution of jobs and wealth due to freer international trade; or liberating changes in human behavior that alarm others who demand a crackdown (such as, in America these days, transgender identity), many people from across the ideological spectrum seem to think that seeking any further expansion in human economic and cultural liberties is a cause best seen as something from a prior age.

Libertarian intellectuals and activists of the sort whose story this book tells would differ strongly, of course, and think that we haven't yet reached any edges we might fall off in pursuit of human liberty, which they maintain still has benefits, both practical and moral, to offer.

Libertarians believe either that people have a *right* to be left alone if they don't harm others or that things will on balance work out *best* that way, generating the most varied and richest culture, or, more commonly, both.

Modern libertarianism is, in many ways, a continuation of the European classical liberalism of the 18th and 19th centuries. Classical liberals of that time believed that free trade made the world richer and more peaceful, that decentralized private-property ownership created a rich and varied spontaneous order, and that legally enforced guilds and aristocracies that lock people into a fixed social status, rather than allow them to live and do business freely, made for an unjust and poorer world. The abolitionist movement that led to the end of slavery in the 19th century was classical liberal to its core, recognizing that all humans should be granted equal rights to obtain and trade property freely, irrespective of national or ethnic background.

Liberalism in that sense meant moving toward greater liberty. In the 20th century, "liberalism"—at least in the English-speaking world; much of continental Europe and Latin America have held fast to its original meaning—has come to mean expanding state power for the (perceived) advancement of social welfare. Some modern libertarians stick closely to that original classical liberal tradition, and some expand it radically: If private property is good, do we need public property? If individual liberty helps us flourish, then why should government regulate our use of drugs or cryptography or weapons, or take from some to benefit others, or make us pay to indoctrinate our children in public schools? The libertarian mission has been to refocus the purpose of politics on that core goal of guaranteeing liberty.

1

Libertarian Ideas before the 20th Century

Libertarianism's all-American roots can be seen in the Declaration of Independence: We're created equal; we tolerate no imposed special privileges. We all have rights to life and to freely seek happiness. Government should help us protect those rights. If it's not doing that, well, it must go.

American government has never lived up to that promise, of course, and Americans did not invent such ideas. You can find libertarianish rhetoric as far back as Confucius's disciple, Mencius, who wrote, "In a nation, the people are the most important, the state is next, and the ruler is the least important."[4]

In the Western tradition, Judaism taught that the king rules beneath God, is subject to His rules, and is not himself divine. Natural rights and natural law traditions recognizing rational standards for behavior and the limits of just government power run through Christian intellectual history.

The English valued their liberties, and Americans were inflamed in their defense of their rights as supposedly free Englishmen by pamphleteers such as John Trenchard and Thomas Gordon, authors of the famous *Cato's Letters.*

Trenchard and Gordon, likely the most widely read pamphleteers of American prerevolutionary times, wrote of natural human rights that came from God and that government must not infringe on—government must merely defend citizens' persons or property. If it exceeds this limited mandate, free men have the right to resist. That's what Americans did, in one of history's first libertarian-inspired revolutions. (And a very rare one—later prominent earth-shaking revolutions, such as those in France and Russia, tried too hard to remake society from the ground up rather than work to restore threatened traditional liberties.) Those ideas about the limits and purpose of government embedded by Thomas Jefferson in the Declaration of Independence were the common air Americans breathed. Explicitly libertarian arguments about whether the Constitution made real or betrayed a libertarian perspective on human freedom also animated leading figures in the anti-slavery movement in mid-19th-century America, such as William Lloyd Garrison and Frederick Douglass.

The modern American libertarian movement also draws on insights from European classical liberals in the 18th and 19th centuries and earlier. As far back as the 16th century, French essayist Étienne de la Boétie explained *how* governments lord over people who always have more force at their command than the government does, in his *Discourse on Voluntary Servitude* (1577). His insight shaped libertarians' mission by recognizing that government's power is ultimately *ideological*, not a matter of massive physical brute force.[5]

People must believe they ought to obey before the state can rule successfully. To raise questions about the state's right to demand such obedience to even its unjust laws and programs, libertarians thus see their mission as casting doubts on the propriety, both moral and practical, of what the state does and how it does it.

From European liberal traditions come such core libertarian concepts as liberty of conscience in matters of belief and religion, the "liberty of the moderns" (freedom to act in one's private and commercial life) versus the liberty of the ancients (ability to be part of political decisionmaking); the abolition of legal class distinctions; free trade; cosmopolitanism; and peace.

The 19th-century figure whose style most shaped modern libertarians is French economist and polemicist Frédéric Bastiat. He followed in the traditions of British free trade advocates Richard Cobden and John Bright, whose writings and advocacy helped lead to the abolition of Britain's Corn Laws—tariffs and restrictions on imported grain—in 1846. That political success for liberalism was understood by economic historians to have increased welfare for people in the bottom 90 percent of income distribution in the United Kingdom.

Freedom of trade was a core concern of Bastiat's, and satire was his chief weapon. He attacked the protectionist logic of mercantilists by showing that it implied that France would be better off if its exports sank at sea before they could be sold, because the profits made would be used to buy imports that made the "balance of trade" "worse." Bastiat wrote an ironic petition of candlemakers against the sun, arguing with impeccable protectionist logic that French industry would benefit if the country barred that economically destructive source of free, imported light.

Bastiat used humane but biting humor to celebrate the abundance markets create, and to mock blinkered protectionist economic policies, which, if rigorously applied, make all our lives less abundant. He directly influenced many

20th-century libertarians with his thinking and his light, humane tone.

The massive mid-19th-century popularity of Herbert Spencer, both in England and America, shows that even radical libertarianism was no unprecedented invention of the 20th-century libertarian movement. In his major work of political philosophy, *Social Statics*, Spencer argued for a law of human nature that should be understood if we want to succeed in society, in the same way that scientific laws must be understood to successfully master nature. His understanding of that "law of equal freedom"—which says that humans should be able to do whatever they wish so long as that freedom does not impede someone else's freedom to do the same—led Spencer to the anarchistic conclusion that we all have a "right of people to ignore the state."[6]

Spencer's influence was so large that he became a target for Supreme Court justice Oliver Wendell Holmes in the 1905 *Lochner* case. That case famously overturned a maximum-working-hours law on economic liberty grounds that Holmes felt were extraconstitutional and influenced by Spencer's libertarianism. Holmes declared in his dissent, "The Fourteenth Amendment does not enact Mr. Herbert Spencer's *Social Statics*."[7] (Holmes elsewhere wrote that no writer but Darwin had done more than Spencer to influence his age's thinking.)[8]

For a variety of complicated reasons, the dominant definitions of "liberalism" and "individualism" shifted in an unlibertarian direction over the first few decades of the 20th century. The full flowering of the individual, the story now went, happened with material security—supposedly—provided by a technocratically managed government that, though it might *seem* to restrict us or manage us, really did for us only what we would do for ourselves, were we able. This change was allegedly more liberating to the individual than the old liberal vision of people free to build spontaneous orders and manage their lives according to their own wills. (The exploration of spontaneous order theory was one of the grand contributions of 20th-century libertarian hero F. A. Hayek.) To the contrary, the classical economists had understood that all sorts of unforeseeable marvels, choices, and wealth would arise from the principle *not* of intelligent management of society, but of laissez faire.

2

Ludwig von Mises and F. A. Hayek

Two of the biggest influences on modern American libertarianism as it coalesced in the 1940s and 1950s, Ludwig von Mises and F. A. Hayek, were economists as well as self-conscious classical liberals. They believed technocratic manipulation of the economy led not toward just equality and prosperity, but toward instability, wealth destruction, and a "road to serfdom." Both were Austrian and representatives of a style of economics still known as "Austrian economics."

The Austrian economics tradition began with the 1871 publication of a book by Carl Menger known in English as *Principles of Economics*.[9] Economics to Menger was about the desires and valuations of individual consumers, which explain the formation of market prices. This approach appeals to the libertarian-minded, as it implies that the best results for everyone arise from allowing the free play of consumer desires to shape what producers produce, what things cost, and what shape the economy should take.

Mises

Ludwig von Mises is rightly seen as the key foundational figure of modern libertarianism. His dominance lies in the depth and influence of his own masterfully detailed explanations and defenses of the principles of 19th-century classical liberalism and free-market economics, as well as in the way his thinking on economics shaped the ideas of later libertarian intellectual giants such as F. A. Hayek, Murray Rothbard, and Ayn Rand. (Though influenced by Mises, they didn't all follow him on every aspect of his thinking.)

Mises was born September 29, 1881, in the Austro-Hungarian city of Lemberg.[10] He received a doctorate in law from the University of Vienna in 1906. His interest in economics began when he read Menger's *Principles*. Menger's vision of the beneficial order of free markets turned him away from the common interventionism of the day and toward classical liberalism.

Mises worked with the Austrian chamber of commerce and lectured at the University of Vienna (not as a salaried employee, but paid directly by his students).[11] He served for three years as an artillery captain at the front during World War I.[12] Then, in 1922, Mises published his first magisterial work, which expanded beyond economics to political philosophy and the social sciences entire, presenting almost every free-market argument he would make from then on.

The book was called *Socialism: An Economic and Sociological Analysis*, and it explained how its titular philosophy was destructive of a happy and rich civilization.[13] F. A. Hayek, the second great Austrian economist who shaped modern libertarianism, worked for Mises as an assistant at the chamber of commerce when the book came out.[14]

Hayek had no idea that

> Mises was also writing the book which would make the most profound impression on my generation . . . a work on political economy in the tradition of the great moral philosophers. . . . There can be no doubt whatever about the effect on us who have been in their most impressionable age. To none of us young men who read the book when it appeared the world was ever the same again.[15]

Socialism's most lasting contribution was Mises's demonstration that socialism in a dynamic industrial economy could never replace the free-market price system's ability to match producers' decisions with consumers' desires. The argument over this proposition—which went back and forth for many years—became known as the "socialist calculation debate."

Socialist economist Oskar Lange once ironically claimed, "A statue of Professor Mises ought to occupy an honorable place in the great hall of the Ministry of Socialization or of the Central Planning Board of the socialist state."[16] Why? Because Mises showed them the problems they had to—and would!—conquer in order to craft a working economic order without the guidance of money prices and the efficiency and incentives that arise from private property.

In the 1920s, after Russia's Bolshevik Revolution, most Western intellectuals saw socialism as a great idea and one that would likely win out over the globe. What private property and prices did that the socialists didn't understand, Mises explained, was reduce comparisons between incommensurable objects to a common denominator—a money price. Without that common denominator, rational and efficient decisions about what to make and in what quantities to meet real and demonstrable human needs were impossible. For instance, what if you possess a warehouse full of steel, but need food to eat? In a market economy, prices tell you what everything is worth in relation to everything else. If steel sells for $120 a pound, and apples for

$3 a pound, you know a pound of steel is worth 40 times more than a pound of apples.

With private property and people's ability to keep the residual profits they earn by buying and selling, market prices likely represent as close as possible at any moment how people actually value things. Why? Because "wrong" prices create entrepreneurial opportunities to raise or lower them until they do reflect people's actual desires. In that process, profit-seeking private-property owners have an incentive to raise or lower their own prices to match people's real desires. This results in a continuous market process that never ends in the modern economists' perfect model of an equilibrium where trading becomes irrelevant. Thus, the combination of prices and private property comes as close as any social process could to reflecting true social desires about what should be made and what it should cost.

Under true socialism in the sense in which Mises used the term (the understood use at the time), one set of government planners owns everything and makes allocation decisions without market prices. In that situation, they'll come nowhere near reflecting people's actual desires. The prevalence of shortages and waste in the Soviet Union before it eventually collapsed helped convince many economists that Mises was right, though few thought so at the time. After the Soviet Union's collapse, though, popular economics journalist

Robert Heilbroner, no fan of Mises, declared in the *New Yorker* the new conventional wisdom: "It turns out, of course, that Mises was right."[17]

Free-market prices, as understood by Austrian theory, spread information about everyone's subjective valuations of what they want and what they are willing to pay for it. In doing so they depend, as Hayek especially emphasized, on unique personal awareness of specific local circumstances that no central planner could ever know, except through the very market prices the planners think they can either eliminate or invent.

After publishing *Socialism*, Mises wrote *Liberalism in the Classical Tradition*, a brilliant and concise explanation of his social and political philosophy. Mises's liberalism is materialistic; "it has nothing else in view than the advancement of [man's] outward, material welfare."[18] It is capitalistic, but recognizes that a truly liberal capitalist system has as its engine not capitalists' whims, but consumers' desires. It is democratic, but only pragmatically so; democracy largely ensures peaceful turnover of state power. It is utilitarian; Mises advocates economic and personal liberty not from a metaphysical belief in rights, but because liberalism delivers the greatest wealth and abundance for all.

His liberalism requires peace for its fullest flowering. Mises argues that a universal liberal order is the only guarantee for international peace. Only when everyone can benefit from everyone else's ideas and productivity through universal free trade can we avoid the grievances and demands for colonialism and *lebensraum* that triggered the 20th century's hideous wars. Mises's liberalism is also a doctrine of maximal tolerance: "Liberalism proclaims tolerance for every religious faith and every metaphysical belief, not out of indifference for these 'higher' things, but from the conviction that the assurance of peace within society must take precedence over everything."[19]

Mises's liberalism is rooted in private property: if property is protected by law, the other aspects of Mises's liberalism will also result. Mises saw his liberalism not as an intellectual innovation, but as a continuation of the dominant liberal philosophy of the 19th century, which had been eclipsed in the 20th by bloody statist doctrines such as socialism and nationalism.

Mises explained in *Epistemological Problems of Economics* the logical connection between economics as he understood it and libertarianism:

> [Before the development of economics,] it had been believed that no bounds other than those drawn by the laws of nature circumscribed the path of acting man. It was not known that there is still something more that sets a limit to political power beyond which

it cannot go. . . . [I]n the social realm too there is something operative which power and force are unable to alter and to which they must adjust themselves if they hope to achieve success.[20]

Thus, government must always remain humble in its goals in the face of economic reality and realize that most attempts to achieve goals through intervention are bound to fail, even by the standards of those who advocated the interventions. For example, those who institute price controls want goods to be abundant and cheap; but such controls inevitably lead to the goods becoming scarce and expensive as people refuse to sell at losses.

Mises fled Austria for Switzerland as the Nazis took over. Seeing the situation in Europe getting grimmer and grimmer, in 1940 he and his wife Margit began the difficult process of legally escaping Europe for the United States. The liberal cause he fought for seemed doomed as Europe was riven by fascism and destruction.

Finding an academic berth commensurate with his high reputation in Europe proved difficult. Mises found new friends in America who recognized his importance and helped him. Most significant was the economics journalist and *New York Times* editorialist Henry Hazlitt—who was already an enormous fan. In his *Times* review of *Socialism*, Hazlitt called it "an economic classic in our time." When he first spoke to Mises on the phone, it felt, he said, as if he had picked up the phone and heard, "This is John Stuart Mill speaking."[21]

Hazlitt became the most successful popularizer of his friend and hero Mises's ideas, most importantly via Hazlitt's book *Economics in One Lesson*. That book, rooted in Frédéric Bastiat's polemical style and thus further linking 20th-century libertarianism with 19th-century classical liberalism, has been a powerful introduction to free-market economic thinking for generations of young proto-libertarians. Hazlitt stressed the central insight of proper economic thinking as trying to notice "things not seen" when it comes to government intervention. For example, the inherent value of government spending is more questionable when you learn to focus not on the visible thing government did with the resources it took via taxation, but on all the unseen things that would have happened had the government not taken the resources, had the valuable thing not been destroyed. Ronald Reagan once told Hazlitt he was "proud to count [him]self as one of your students."[22] Hazlitt reached enormous audiences for two decades with his free-market opinion column in *Newsweek*, which ran from 1946 to 1966.

Mises's major work during his first decade in America was a nearly 900-page detailed explanation of every aspect of economic science, *Human Action: A Treatise on Economics*, published by Yale University Press in 1948. Fellow travelers in the nascent American libertarian movement saw it as exactly what they needed. One individualist critic, Rose Wilder Lane, wrote that the book "begins and will stand for a new epoch in human thought, therefore in human action and world history."[23] Hazlitt in his *Newsweek* column called it "a landmark in the progress of economics. . . . If a single book can turn the ideological tide that has been running in recent years so heavily toward statism, socialism, and totalitarianism, *Human Action* is that book. It should become the leading text of everyone who believes in . . . a free-market economy."[24]

After explaining the hows and whys of economic concepts such as marginal utility, price formation, the division of labor, and profit and loss, Mises analyzed the (always bad) effects of government interventions, ranging from taxation to price and foreign exchange controls, to restricting production and expanding credit, and even to legal tender legislation.

His analysis in *Human Action* is consistently value free; Mises demonstrates that government interventions fail to achieve their goals *on the terms of those who desire them*. Mises also points out that a failed government intervention contains the roots of *more* intervention. Government bureaucrats stubbornly continue to try to achieve their desired result through more interventions that also fail, spinning more and more complex webs of ineffective controls. That dynamic made him deny the possibility of a viable "third way" between free markets and socialism; once you start down the road to the latter, you tend to stay on it.

Hayek

That was also the theme of the most famous popular work of Mises's student and the most influential member of the Austrian school of economics, F. A. Hayek. His decades of work covered economics, intellectual history, cognitive science, and evolutionary biology, and he remains among the most respected of libertarian thinkers in academia.

He also directly influenced politicians. Former British prime minister Margaret Thatcher once visited her Conservative Party's research division and, thinking they were too timid in moving faster toward freer markets, pulled out Hayek's *The Constitution of Liberty* and slammed it down, informing her colleagues, "This is what we believe."[25]

Hayek was born in Vienna on May 8, 1899. The young Hayek was not a great student, though he did seem to have some bent toward science as he followed his father's interest in plant classification. In World War I, he joined a field artillery unit for Austria-Hungary and was sent to the Piave River front in Italy. He saw little fighting, but contracted malaria. In the military, he encountered his first economics texts, which were so bad in his judgment that he said, "I still marvel that the particular books did not give me a permanent distaste for the subject."[26]

After the war, he earned two doctorates from the University of Vienna, one in law in 1921, the other in political science in 1923. In Vienna, he studied under Friedrich von Wieser, leader of the second generation of Mengerian/"Austrian" economics. Hayek's first professional job was at the Austrian Office of Claims Accounts, working under Mises, star of that tradition's third generation. Hayek first learned from Mises why socialism doesn't work—a lesson Hayek spread even more widely than his mentor.

In 1927, Hayek launched the Austrian Institute for Business Cycle Research. (Mises helped with fundraising.) Hayek directed the organization, with funding from the Rockefeller Foundation and later some help from game theory innovator Oskar Morgenstern.[27]

While running the institute, he began lecturing in economics at the University of Vienna in 1929.[28] His continued fascination with the cause and cure of business cycles spurred both his professional success and his storied, heated clash with his personal friend and intellectual adversary, John Maynard Keynes, the most influential economist of the 20th century.

The clash occurred in and among the faculty at the London School of Economics, where Hayek began teaching in 1931.[29] The Hayek-Keynes battle lines were drawn over, among other issues, whether one could cure business cycle–generated unemployment via manipulating "aggregate demand"—government attempts to give consumers more, or less, purchasing power as government planners thought expedient. They also dueled over whether society-wide saving and investment can drift out of balance through any means other than an artificial—and generally state-driven—expansion of bank credit.

Hayek's Austrian business cycle theory maintained that if banks, or governments, artificially lowered interest rates without that matching a real desire for more production or consumption of goods in the future, people would tend to invest in long-term projects that would prove uneconomical, ultimately leading to unemployment and capital consumption. This was the "bust" following the "boom" caused by government's inflationary policy of artificially boosting money and credit. The libertarian implication is that government officials should dispense with the belief that they can solve economic problems via manipulative fiscal and monetary policy, since such interventions cause other unsustainable economic problems in the long run. Keynes, for his part, thought unemployment was caused by insufficient aggregate demand and could be lowered by pumping in the money that Hayek saw as ultimately disruptive. Keynes's goal, Hayek insisted, was to trick workers into acquiescing to a real wage cut through inflation that they would not tolerate if they knew it was happening.[30]

During World War II, in a world wracked with violence by totalitarian states, Hayek crafted the 20th-century nonfiction libertarian work that has had the widest reach and impact: *The Road to Serfdom*, an apologia for old-fashioned liberalism against the then-current mania for planning and socialism in the West.[31] *Serfdom* has sold over a quarter million copies in its English-language edition and has been translated into more than 20 foreign languages—counting only authorized versions. Underground translations in Russian, Czech, and Polish brought Hayek's vital message about economic and political liberty behind the Iron Curtain before it fell. Russian occupying authorities in postwar Berlin tried to ban its import into East Germany, but tenacious admirers of Western liberty smuggled in copies that were clandestinely reproduced and spread. Upon its 1944 release, it was a surprising popular success, and it was even condensed and reprinted in

America's bible of periodicals at the time, *Reader's Digest*, a magazine then read by more than three million Americans, consisting of edited excerpts from other magazines and books and some original content.[32] Hayek was swept against his expectations, and almost against his will, on a whirlwind publicity and polemical tour. The quiet, abstract economist and philosopher found himself suddenly famous in America.

Hayek's defense of individualism and liberty is not based on a belief in human grandeur or ability. It's based rather on our limits and weakness, particularly the limits and weakness of our reason. Hayek stressed not the state's moral evil, but its blindness: the insurmountable limits of what states could accomplish in accordance with their own goals, which are necessarily circumscribed by the limits of man's reason and knowledge.

Hayek summarized his own contribution like this: "What I had done had often seemed to me more to point out barriers to further advance on the path chosen by others than to supply new ideas which opened the path to further development."[33]

Serfdom warned that central economic planning, no matter how well-meaning, tended toward a loss of most liberties. It was a warning to the Allied nations about to inherit the world after the defeat of the Axis that the hated Nazis were rooted in the same sort of economic planning then embraced by the

Westerners fighting them. He acknowledged that the road is a slower, drearier trudge than the Nazis' but thought the final destination to be the same.

Some of Hayek's foes reduced his book's message to an easily disproved absurdity—that any socialism leads swiftly and inevitably to complete tyranny. Hayek said in a 1976 introduction to a reissue of the book: "It has frequently been alleged that I have contended that any movement in the direction of socialism is bound to lead to totalitarianism. Even though this danger exists, this is not what the book says. What it contains is a warning that unless we mend the principles of our policy, some very unpleasant consequences will follow which most of those who advocate these policies do not want."

Serfdom was a revelation to a generation for whom classical liberalism was a forgotten anachronism. In it, Hayek defends the information-transmitting powers of the free price system—a way for everyone everywhere to understand the collective subjective desires and to use the collective knowledge of everyone else, even when scattered individuals might not even be able to articulate those things themselves. In its pages, Hayek also

- Delimits the power of democracy;

- Defends the rule of law over the arbitrary rule of men;

- Explains how total economic control leads to total political control;

- Details how unequal market rewards inform people how they can best serve the good of all society;

- Insists that leaders of a fully planned society will tend toward jingoistic nationalism and dubious moral virtue;

- Shows how planning inspires a tendency toward government thought control; and

- Provides the intellectual history of how Nazism grew from socialism, rather than being, as many believed, a capitalist *reaction to* socialism.

Despite its importance to libertarianism, *Serfdom* is not a total condemnation of government's role. The powers Hayek grants rightfully to government include restricting production methods, as long as such laws are enforced fairly and equally and are known in advance so people can adjust their plans to the regulations. He approves of sanitary laws, working-hour laws, disaster relief, government provision of certain social services, and a welfare state that would provide a minimum standard of living for all. His standard of the proper working economy is "competition," not laissez faire.

Although Hayek had served as an influential counterbalance to Keynes during the early 1930s, by the end of World War II Keynesian ideas—which were conducive to government's trying to manage the economy—had won the day. After World War II, Hayek mostly abandoned technical economics for political philosophy, history, and a foray into theoretical neurology in *The Sensory Order* (1952).

3

Founding Mothers

The year before Hayek's *Serfdom* hit the world, three women—each a combination of novelist and political philosopher, each appalled at seeing America's promise of unbridled, glorious individualism being betrayed—brought to bear, quite effectively, their own moral, literary, and historical weapons in the war against collectivism and statism.

The modern American libertarian movement could convincingly be credited to the intellectual efforts of those three women—all friends, at least for a time. Their first major works on political and ideological matters all appeared in 1943, with America embroiled in wartime centralization. As individualist-friendly journalist John Chamberlain put it: "It was three women—Mrs. [Isabel] Paterson, Rose Wilder Lane, and Ayn Rand—who, with scornful side glances at the male business community, had decided to rekindle a faith in an older American philosophy. There wasn't an economist among them. And none of them was a Ph.D."[34]

Rand's 1943 classic was her third novel, though only her first successful one, *The Fountainhead*; Lane's was *The Discovery of Freedom: Man's Struggle against Authority* and Paterson's *The God of the Machine*. Before these works, free-market and libertarian-leaning ideas had nearly disappeared except for a scattered few journalists and polemicists who were later labeled the "Old Right"—the American political right before the Cold War made fighting communism the dominant concern of people known as conservatives. Among the Old Right (again, a designation of later historians, not their own self-identification) were H. L. Mencken (in the 1920s one of the most influential critics and thinkers in the country, especially among college-age intellectuals), Albert Jay Nock, Garet Garrett, and some writers associated with publications such as the *Saturday Evening Post* and the *Chicago Tribune*.

Isabel Paterson

Paterson, though little read or remembered today, established in many ways the tone, content, and style of modern libertarian argumentation. *The God of the Machine* was the former novelist and literary critic's one work of political philosophy. In it, she explained American exceptionalism and explored why this country was so uniquely prosperous, and in doing so, staked out a set of positions on economics and politics that have defined the libertarian movement ever since.

Paterson was a native Canadian, born Isabel Bowler. She spent her girlhood in the American West, farming, ranching, and communing with Native Americans. She had only two and a half years of formal education, but she educated herself by reading widely and constantly.

Without ascribing undue virtue to the frontierspeople she knew as a youth, she saw that, as her biographer Stephen Cox wrote, "frontier society offered 'the most civilized type of association' . . . because it had 'the absolute minimum of external regulation' and therefore 'the maximum of voluntary civility and morality.' . . . What worked out West wasn't aggressiveness but 'a peculiarly individual, mind-your-own-business confidence.'"[35] She deliberately emulated those qualities.

In 1910, she married a Canadian real estate agent named Kenneth Birrell Paterson. Within a year, however, they were no longer living together, according to evidence found by her biographer, and by 1918 they were so estranged, though not divorced officially, that she apparently had no idea what had become of him.[36] Through the 1910s, Paterson became a newspaperwoman in New York and in the Pacific Northwest, producing editorials and drama criticism. She published her first novel, *The Shadow Riders*, in 1916. In 1921, a mutual friend introduced her to Burton Rascoe, then literary editor of the *New York Tribune* (later the *New York Herald Tribune*).

Paterson became an influential literary critic from her berth at the *Herald Tribune*, with a cheeky, biting reputation. She wrote a weekly column in the paper's Books supplement, called "Turns with a Bookworm."

As with most individualists and proto-libertarians of her day, President Franklin D. Roosevelt and his New Deal frustrated her. Drawing on analysis from Old Right journalist Garet Garrett and her own independent thinking, she concluded that government policies, particularly efforts to keep commodity prices high in the 1920s, led to the Great Depression, and that the Depression persisted largely because of governments' own efforts to end it.

She was appalled at the degree to which all respectable literary intellectuals in the 1930s avidly embraced state planning. She peppered her columns throughout the 1930s and early 1940s with the political ideas later fully developed in *God of the Machine*. Critic and novelist Edmund Wilson reacted to her political commentary by telling her she was "the last surviving person to believe in those quaint old notions on which the republic was founded."[37] (The sense that every libertarian in the 1940s was unique was common both among them and among often perplexed observers. This was a *very* unknown ideology then.)

Paterson had become friends with two other individualist women, novelists Rose Wilder Lane and Ayn Rand, with whom she could speak sympathetically on her political beliefs. Both learned much from Paterson.

Alarmed at the parlous state of Western civilization, she intended for *God of the Machine* to explain what made it so precious and rare. It was published by G. P. Putnam's Sons in 1943, and was a commercial failure, though it has continued to float back into print over the years because of interest on the part of some small ideological publishers. The book's title, as her biographer Cox wrote, could be interpreted to possibly mean human intelligence, which is what powers the machine economy, or possibly God himself, "the original 'Source of energy' for the human dynamo and the guarantor of the principles from which human liberty proceeds."[38]

The book was built around envisioning human society as a machine of sorts. The healthiest and wealthiest of cultures, said Paterson, had built the most elaborate and stable "long circuit" energy systems, which ran on "absolute security of private property, full personal liberty, and firm autonomous regional bases for a federal structure."[39]

Her metaphors were mechanical, but her philosophy was not materialist. Of the Romans, she writes: "Neither their location nor their material progress, no economic clue, accounts for their function. . . . What the past shows . . . is that the imponderables outweigh every material article. . . . Nations are not powerful because they possess wide lands, safe ports, large navies, huge armies, fortifications, stores, money, and credit. They acquire those advantages because they are powerful, having devised on correct principles the political structure which allows the flow of energy to take its proper course."[40]

Paterson tried to demonstrate how America became the wealthiest and most powerful nation in history by most closely approximating those proper ideas for structuring human society. Those include classical republicanism above pure democracy (because the latter allows rights or property to be violated merely by majority rule); identifies slavery as the "fault in the structure" the Founders built; and radically assaults the growth in government since the Progressive Era and the New Deal.

In *God of the Machine*, Paterson condemns antitrust law, argues that the right to produce and exchange freely is core to basic human existence, and insists that if one permits public ownership of property, a society will soon experience "long trains of prisoners transported in cattle cars to a place where they do not wish to go."[41]

Libertarian theorists insist that liberty manifestly has both ethical and practical advantages. Why do so many people fail to realize this? Paterson offered an answer, in the chapter most remembered among libertarians, brutally titled "The Humanitarian with the Guillotine." She concludes: "If the primary objective of the philanthropist, his justification for living, is to help others, his ultimate goal *requires that others shall be in want.* His happiness is the obverse of their misery. If he wishes to help 'humanity,' the whole of humanity must be in need. The humanitarian wishes to be a prime mover in the lives of others. He cannot admit either the divine or the natural order, by which men have the power to help themselves."[42]

Paterson believed private charity, though admittedly "random and sporadic" and unable to "prevent suffering completely," at least doesn't "perpetuate the dependence of its beneficiaries" and keeps deprivation from spreading too widely—at least in a culture enough in command of the long-circuit energy system to be wealthy. The United States, she notes, is "the only country on record that has never had a famine since it became a nation."[43]

But charity pales in comparison to the most helpful thing a person can do for another person: launch an enterprise that can employ that person and allow him or her to survive. Paterson notes:

> If the full roll of *sincere* philanthropists were called, from the beginning of time, it would be found that all of them together by their strictly philanthropic activities have never conferred upon humanity one-tenth of the benefit derived from the normally self-interested efforts of Thomas Alva Edison, to say nothing of the greater minds who worked out the scientific principles which Edison applied.[44]

Although the book did distressingly poorly and ended Paterson's career as a writer of books, her other founding libertarian friends saw what she accomplished, and loved it. Rose Wilder Lane wrote to her pen pal, the former president Herbert Hoover, "It seems to me a book ranking with the best of Paine and Madison."[45] In her review of the book, Lane insisted that "anyone who has read it comfortably has not read it adequately, and should read it again and again until he experiences an earthquake."[46] Ayn Rand believed that Paterson's book "does for capitalism what *Das Kapital* did for the Reds" and "what the Bible did for Christianity."[47]

Rand was Paterson's most influential libertarian disciple. She was not usually one to acknowledge intellectual debts to anyone but Aristotle, but Rand told Paterson in a letter: "You were the very first person to see how Capitalism *works* in specific application. That is your achievement, which I consider a historical achievement of the first importance. . . . I learned *from you* the historical and economic aspects of Capitalism."[48]

By the end of the 1940s, Paterson's heterodox politics cost her the *Herald Tribune* column. She failed to sell her last novel. When Paterson died on January 10, 1960, she and her work were at the time largely forgotten. Like her friend Rose Wilder Lane, she refused to take money from Social Security.[49]

Rose Wilder Lane

Rose Wilder Lane, while also little remembered compared with Rand, has a contested claim to literary fame even greater than Rand's, even though Rand has sold tens of millions of novels. Lane's mother was Laura Ingalls Wilder, author of the generation-spanning hit series of novels of frontier life beginning with *Little House on the Prairie*. Some Wilder scholars think Lane's role (Lane was already a successful novelist) in "editing" her mother's novels rose to the level of ghostwriting.

Lane undoubtedly lived part of the American adventure her mother wrote about. Lane, author of the 1943 libertarian classic

The Discovery of Freedom, was born on December 5, 1886, in De Smet, in the South Dakota Territory. She was the only child of Almanzo and Laura Ingalls Wilder to survive past infancy. Her early years were a hardscrabble settler's life not unlike her mother's childhood, which was the subject of the *Little House* books.

Rose began living unconventionally—compared with what was expected of a young woman in the early 20th century—early on. She worked as a Western Union telegraph operator in Kansas City and Indiana, then drifted out to San Francisco where she had a short marriage to traveling salesman Claire Gillette Lane. In 1909, she miscarried; by 1916, she was no longer living with him, though their formal divorce took another couple of years, and she retained Lane's name.[50] (This situation closely resembled Paterson's—a youthful marriage to a man whose name she retained but with whom she lived only briefly.)

After years of bohemian living and journalism in San Francisco, socializing with young Reds and thinking of herself as one of them, Lane made her way to Europe in 1920 under the auspices of the Red Cross. She spent much of the rest of the decade venturing across Europe and parts of the Middle East, usually with close female friends, including Dorothy Thompson, a young journalist who later married Sinclair Lewis and became an influential newspaper columnist.

By the end of the 1920s, a somewhat resentful Lane ended up living in the Ozarks at Rocky Ridge, caring for her parents. Lane had built up a nest egg writing popular fiction in the 1920s, but her fortune disappeared in the 1929 stock market crash. During the 1930s she stayed at Rocky Ridge and began her editing, collaboration, or possibly ghostwriting, of her mother's series of children's books. The *Little House* books show signs of Lane's passion for liberty; Lane's biographer William Holtz draws attention to a sequence in *Little House* set on the Fourth of July in which young Laura decides that "Americans won't obey any king on earth" and when she is grown "there isn't anyone else who has a right to give me orders."[51]

Rose was a prominent literary voice in the *Saturday Evening Post* of the 1930s, which was then one of the more popular places to find anti–New Deal sentiment under the editorship of George Horace Lorimer. Lane began working occasionally with Old Right journalist Garet Garrett; she toured farming country alongside him for a *Saturday Evening Post* article. Rose hated the restrictions imposed on American farmers by New Deal policies. By 1935, this former socialist wrote in the *Post*, "I am now a fundamentalist American, give me time and I will tell you why individualism, laissez-faire, and the slightly restrained anarchy of capitalism offers the best possibilities for the development of the human spirit."[52]

Lane explained her new Americanism in a popular *Post* article titled "Credo," published in March 1936.[53] This article inspired Los Angeles Chamber of Commerce manager Leonard Read (more on him shortly) to launch a publishing imprint with some friends called Pamphleteers Inc., to republish Lane's essay under the title "Give Me Liberty."[54]

Disillusioned by the state of freedom in the United States, and with her mother flush with money because of the *Little House* books, Rose bought a farmhouse in Danbury, Connecticut, where she lived out the rest of her days.

Both Lane and Paterson were popular novelists making their first forays into nonfiction. Both took a world-historical view, and both tried to explain how liberty primed the unprecedented prosperity of mid-20th-century America. Both built overarching metaphors: for Paterson, society is a machine and the US Constitution is a "mechanical drawing" for a society "amazing in its correctness, in respect of the relation of mass and motion, operative through the association of human beings, and the release and application of energy"; for Lane, "human energy" is fully accessible only when men are individual and free: "This is the nature of human energy; individuals generate it, and control it. Each person is self-controlling, and therefore responsible for his acts. Every human being, *by his nature*, is free."[55]

The Discovery of Freedom is concerned with the glories of, and best path toward, human growth and change. Lane's vision centers on the power of ideas—nothing about the laws of human nature changed to make America unique; the change was ideological. Americans realized the power of free human energy more than other cultures in human history had.

Lane's ideology seems largely self-created, aside from what she learned from Paterson; *Discovery* has few references to past thinkers. Economic controls cause the fall of great nations, she argues. She writes of three past attempts to build a culture on the notion, in her eyes, that man is and must be free: the biblical Israelites, the Saracen (Muslim) empire in the centuries after Muhammad, and the United States. She credits the biblical Israelis with the first realization that man was free and the Saracens with creating the first technologically sophisticated, scientific civilization. The European Renaissance, she argues, came from Italy's exposure to the Saracen world.

Discovery is an eccentric and spirited contribution to a specific strain of the modern libertarian character: historically visionary, rooted in American experience yet foreseeing a world transformed by a political and ideological spirit that should be universal. She stresses the essentially murderous nature of government controls—to Lane, both American and world history provide abundant lessons leading to the conclusion that only laissez faire can allow humanity to keep thriving.

In her later days, Lane wrote a postcard to a radio host condemning Social Security as an example of the kind of socialist paternalism that Americans supposedly fought to eliminate in World War II. A postmaster thought he detected something seditious in this sort of opinion and called in the FBI, who sent a young state police officer to look into this old lady's strange views. Lane asked him if that opinion was considered subversive. He said, "Yes, ma'am, it was." Lane thundered back: "Then I'm subversive as all hell! . . . I say this, and I write this, and I broadcast it on the radio, and I'm going to keep right on doing it 'til you put me in jail. Write that down and report it to your superiors!" Canned vegetables and slaughtered pigs, she said, were the only *true* form of social security.[56]

Lane was an early movement-conscious libertarian, following the activities of student groups like those led by her protégé Roger MacBride—later a Libertarian Party (LP) presidential candidate—and commiserating with movement financier Jasper Crane of DuPont Chemical on his ultimately failed attempts to launch a free-market economics journal to be run by Hans Sennholz, a student of Ludwig von Mises's, or an academy to teach only free-market economics. In a 1947 letter to

Crane, she uses the phrase "libertarian movement" to identify those who shared her politics, possibly the first use of the term in its modern sense. She encouraged the young because as she saw it, the philosophy of individualism "hasn't had its Plato yet. I'm betting that the oncoming youngsters will produce one."[57]

Lane wrote to Crane in 1958:

Twenty years ago, do you remember? It was almost impossible to find *one* [other libertarian]. I used to spend all my time, every day, at my typewriter following up every least little "lead" that I could find. Example: I heard a high-school "debate" among all pro–New Dealers on the radio, and wrote to each of them. One replied, with all the Welfare State collectivist notions that had been put into his head, but he didn't seem wholly unintelligent, so I kept on writing to him for some months, apparently with no effect, finally getting no answer. Now he turns up as publisher of *National Review*, telling people that I—i.e., my letters—changed his whole life. . . . The whole "climate of opinion" is changing. And every least little thing that you have done has helped to change it; never think that a bit of it failed, even when it seemed to.[58]

Lane's faith in the American character and the unleashed energy of free people made her "as certain as anyone can be of anything in the future that the twentieth century will end as the eighteenth did, with a great revival and resurgence of individualism."[59]

It did, and a lot of credit for that can go to Lane's and Paterson's friend Ayn Rand.

Ayn Rand

Ayn Rand is undoubtedly the most influential libertarian of the 20th century to a mass public, with her ideological advocacy launched through popular novels. She has had tens of millions of paying readers, whose passion for her is huge: When the publisher Modern Library did a reader's poll of top 100 novels in 1998, the top two slots both went to Rand, for *The Fountainhead* and *Atlas Shrugged*. Her works continue to sell in the hundreds of thousands every year.[60]

Unlike the great libertarian economists Mises, Hayek, and Milton Friedman, Rand didn't think she was continuing, building on, and refining the classical liberal tradition. She believed she was recreating philosophy from the ground up. Her political libertarianism was based on more than understanding that laissez faire capitalism created more wealth than the alternatives, or even that freedom was a positive good.

Rand's philosophy, which she called Objectivism, was a unified structure with ontology and epistemology at its root, with politics and ethics both distant derivations thereof. She tended to hold in contempt those who reached libertarian political conclusions without her Objectivist philosophy as a foundation. Thus, despite her central role as an influence on and shaper of libertarian thought and activism, she famously denied even *being* a libertarian. But her politics were libertarian, and since libertarianism writ large does *not* demand the sort of extrapolitical superstructure she insisted on for Objectivism, Ayn Rand, whether she admitted it or not, was a libertarian, one of the most important ever.

Rand—including her name—was self-made. She was born Alissa Rosenbaum on February 2, 1905, in Saint Petersburg, Russia, to shop-owning chemist Fronz Rosenbaum and his wife Anna. She lived through the bloody chaos of the Russian Revolution and saw her family's future, and any ability for the individual to freely craft his or her own life and joy through his or her own choices and property, ruthlessly crushed or stolen. She knew she had to escape.

After years of trying, and with the help of relatives in Chicago, Rand got a rare passport out of Russia in 1926. She was supposed to visit her American relations and then return to the motherland, but she knew nothing could make her return to that tomb of a nation. For years after, she'd tell of how someone approached her at her farewell party, pleading, "If they ask you, in America—tell them that Russia is a huge cemetery and that we are all dying slowly." "I'll tell them," Rand remembers promising.[61]

The young Alissa, using the name Ayn Rand in America, didn't start with an ambition to found a philosophic or political movement. She adored American movies, finding in them a rare emotional fuel when she managed to see one in Russia. They embodied her fantasies about the wonderland to which she longed to escape: wealthy, romantic, free. She wanted to be part of that tradition.

In an appropriately Romantic twist, Rand ran into the famous director Cecil B. DeMille by accident on his studio lot in Culver City after moving to Los Angeles. The awestruck Russian girl charmed him and soon became a regular extra on his sets, where she met another extra who became her husband, a midwestern boy named Frank O'Connor also trying to make his way in the film business. She moved up to reviewing literary properties for DeMille while working on her own apprentice screenplays and novels.

Her first published novel was *We the Living* (1935), set in Soviet Russia and emphasizing its misery and tyranny. She believed principles were more important than specifics.

Thus, her theme was not just that the Soviet Union was a hellish nightmare, but that collectivism anywhere is the enemy of the human spirit.

Rand knew by 1934 whom she intended to become. She had sent H. L. Mencken—the leading individualist voice of the 1920s and the last such to achieve popularity and distinction in America before the rise of the modern libertarian movement—a prepublication copy of the *We the Living* manuscript and credited him with being "the greatest representative of a philosophy to which I want to dedicate my whole life." She continued:

> I have always regarded you as the foremost champion of individualism in this country. . . . Perhaps it may seem a lost cause at present, and there are those who will say that I am too late, that I can only hope to be the last fighter for a mode of thinking which has no place in the future. But I do not think so. I intend to be the first one in a new battle which the world needs as it has never needed before, the first to answer the many—too many—advocates of collectivism, and answer them in a manner which will not be forgotten.[62]

It took decades, but Rand did what she had promised.

We the Living flopped, released in a very left-leaning decade in American culture. Rand kept herself barely afloat with screenplays and plays for the rest of the decade, then wrote a short science fiction fable called *Anthem*. *Anthem* became her first real connection with others in the burgeoning libertarian movement when, after initially being published only in the United Kingdom, it was discovered in 1945 by Leonard Read—who shortly thereafter was the founder of the first modern libertarian think tank, the Foundation for Economic Education. Set in a future tyranny where individualism is suppressed and everyone is known by number rather than name, in which one man discovers both electricity and the meaning of the word "I," *Anthem* is unlike anything else Rand wrote, a quirky presentation of her philosophic sense of life in fable form. Leonard Read published it in America under his Pamphleteers imprint, which had also published Rose Wilder Lane's *Give Me Liberty*.

In New York City in the early 1940s, Rand worked on what was to become her first mass success, her 1943 individualist classic *The Fountainhead*. During that time, she met and socialized with others in the rare, and then becoming rarer, anti–New Deal, free-market crowd—Paterson most importantly, though Lane was also a friend. She advocated for a specific movement consciousness on the part of fellow individualists and planned, along with drama critic Channing Pollock, a new national organization of individualists.

She wrote a manifesto for such a planned group in 1941. The pro-free-market businesspeople whom she and Pollock tried to recruit doubted that such a new group pushing what they tended to think of as "Americanism" was necessary—didn't the National Association of Manufacturers already stand up for free markets? Rand wrote to Pollock explaining how she saw the situation for individualists then:

> What organization of our side has defined a concrete ideology of Americanism? None. The first aim of our organization will be intellectual and philosophical— not merely political and economic. We will give people . . . a positive, clear and consistent system of belief. Who had done that? Certainly not the [National Association of Manufacturers]. They—and all other organizations—are merely fighting for the system of private enterprise and their entire method consists of teaching and clarifying the nature of that system. . . . We want to teach people, not what the system of private enterprise is, but why we should believe in it and

fight for it. We want to provide a spiritual, ethical, philosophical groundwork for the belief in the system of private enterprise.[63]

While still a struggling novelist, she saw her role as a radical for capitalism.

It took Rand 12 rejections to finally find a publisher for *The Fountainhead*. The book went on to sell well over four million copies and has been in print ever since, still selling tens of thousands of copies a year. Although it was fiction, it was designed to, and did, serve as an initial volley in the political and ideological war for individualism.

The novel details the careers of two architects, the individualist and heroic Howard Roark and the uncreative, spineless Peter Keating. Roark's and Keating's lives cross paths from college on as Roark launches an erratic career, too good and too original for most potential customers, sometimes staying alive by toiling in quarries.

Rand believed that liberty was threatened not just by those openly advocating political tyranny, but by anyone damaging the foundation of individual greatness. Rand contended that evil was inherently powerless, and only won by the acquiescence or cravenness of the potentially good. Thus, Ellsworth Toohey, the great villain of *The Fountainhead*, is not a politician but a critic who dedicated his career to destroying belief in all standards artistic, literary, and political. Villain and hero meet only once: Toohey, eager with curiosity, asks what Roark thinks of him. Roark replies, "But I don't think of you."[64]

The novel ends with a bravura Romantic Randian moment. Roark is on trial for blowing up an (unoccupied) housing project that he designed. The design was corrupted in violation of his agreement with the builder. He convinces the jury he was in the right after telling them:

> I wished to come here and say that the integrity of a man's creative work is of greater importance than any charitable endeavor. Those of you who do not understand this are the men who're destroying the world. . . . I recognize no obligations toward men except one: to respect their freedom and to take no part in a slave society.[65]

The Fountainhead became a slow but eventually huge success, although Rand thought the reviews mostly didn't get what she was trying to do, and even the publisher's advertising evaded the novel's controversial individualist themes. Rand believed in art as a self-standing absolute. She also believed, as she wrote in her journal: "Capitalist democracy has no ideology. That is what this book has to give it."[66] She was hurt that no business or supposedly free-market interest group stood up for the novel.

In 1944, Ayn Rand had returned to Hollywood and to screenwriting, including for a movie version of *The Fountainhead* itself. She socialized occasionally with a crowd of Southern California individualist businesspeople, among them Leonard Read, then the general manager of the Los Angeles Chamber of Commerce. Read would carry on the revolution launched in its modern form in the first half of the 1940s by the two Austrian economists and these three women. He created the institutional framework for that revolution in 1946, when he founded the first educational think tank pushing what he called "the freedom philosophy"— which was directly inspired by all of them.

4

The Foundation for Economic Education

Leonard Read had served in World War I as a mechanic in the aviation section of the Army Signal Corps, then joined hundreds of thousands of his fellow midwesterners in a move to California. He went into real estate and joined the chamber of commerce in Burlingame, a small town between Palo Alto and San Francisco. In 1939, he became general manager of the chamber's Los Angeles branch.

Read initially believed in Roosevelt and the New Deal; that was what decent Americans did at the time. Even the chamber of commerce, that reputed holdout of old-school middle-class pro-business values, tried to go along with National Industrial Recovery Act codes and other strictures of the New Deal's fresh economic controls. By 1943, the chamber's new president announced, "Only the willfully blind can fail to see that . . . [t]he capitalism which . . . fought against justified public regulation of the competitive system is a thing of the past."[67]

Read could not abide this. In the mid-1930s, on chamber business, Read met William C. Mullendore, a former assistant to Herbert Hoover during his secretary of commerce days, who was then vice president of the electric utility Southern California Edison. The blunt and zealous Mullendore changed Read's life by explaining all the ways in which Roosevelt's alphabet soup of agencies repeatedly violated the principles of America's Constitution and would be the economic and moral ruin of our nation.

Under Mullendore's influence, Read wrote a popular anti–New Deal book in 1937, *The Romance of Reality*, which highlighted anti–central control ideas from Herbert Spencer, William Graham Sumner, and Old Right stalwart Albert Jay Nock. Through Read, Mullendore laid the groundwork for the first modern libertarian think tank.

Read realized that refuting the arguments for specific government interventions was like refuting that the earth is square—all fine and good, but until you had explained patiently what the earth is really shaped like, a huge number of false notions would require individual refutation first.

Thus, batting down false principles wasn't good enough; he had to educate people on true ones.

The tiny, scattered gang of 1940s libertarians all managed to find one another, somehow. Read had begun to correspond eagerly with Rose Wilder Lane and became pals with Rand. Read's work with the chamber of commerce and his growing passion for defending the free-market cause in any venue earned him admiration and friendship from a string of businesspeople small and large across the country, who were still doubtful, confused, and concerned about the New Deal, war socialism, and its possible aftermath.

Read left the chamber and hoped he could fight collectivism more strongly at the National Industrial Conference Board (NICB), a nonprofit business membership and research organization founded in 1916 (since renamed the Conference Board).[68] But the NICB had a policy that in educational events it sponsored, to maintain its aura of fairness, "both sides" of any given politico-economic issue should be presented. Read thought, according to his biographer Mary Homan Sennholz:

> The "other side" was everywhere—in government, education, and communications. Even businessmen had come to rely on government for restrictions of competition, for government contracts and orders,

easy money and credit, and other favors. . . . How do you represent "both sides" when "one side" is all around you, preempting the public discussion. . . . How do you state your case for individual freedom and the private property order when the other side is monopolizing the stage?[69]

Read quit the NICB after less than a year. *He* needed to be in charge if he was to be an effective proselytizer for what he called "the freedom philosophy." War socialism and its awful aftermath left him heartily discouraged; after the atom bomb was dropped, Read wrote to a friend:

Savagery returns in a more frightful manner than . . . has ever been known. At a time when bandits are rising to power and when the banditry even in the good of us is manifesting itself we would have to discover the most destructive device ever known to man. Had I been the president of this country and obligated to announce what we had done I would have released to the press only a copy of my prayer asking forgiveness.[70]

In early 1946, Read began raising money and gathering a board of trustees for a new institution, his Foundation for Economic Education (FEE). He found support from manufacturers small and large, insurance magnates, steel barons, car makers, banks, and privately owned electric utilities.

Read wanted FEE to educate for liberty on multiple levels: to publish individualist classics of the Frédéric Bastiat variety to make sure they stayed in print and received wide and, if necessary, free distribution; and to reach out to all Americans—students, industrialists, shopkeepers, and even, if they wanted to listen, politicians. He wanted an organization that would bang the drum in all styles and formats for the eternal value of encouraging "anything that's peaceful"—the title of one of Read's most enduring homiletic essay collections. The FEE message, as Read put it, was to let "anyone do anything he pleases that's peaceful or creative; let there be no organized restraint against anything but fraud, violence, misrepresentation, predation . . . limit society's agency of organized force—government—to juridical and policing functions, tabulating the do-nots and prescribing the penalties against unpeaceful actions; let the government do this and leave all else to the free, unfettered market!"[71]

The real problem with postwar America, Read believed, was that neither politicians nor populace truly grasped the intricacies of free-market economics and therefore didn't perceive that state intervention in peaceful interactions, both personal and economic, was not only counterproductive, but just plain wrong.

He launched FEE in July 1946 with healthy funding, in a mansion on seven acres in Irvington-on-Hudson, New York. By the end of his first year, he had received about $254,000—nearly $2.5 million in current dollars.[72]

When asked how FEE was doing financially, Read liked to declare that its finances couldn't be any better, because, after all, it was getting all the money that people freely chose to give it. When someone would write to tell him they were going to stop their support, he was known to reply:

> I am pleased that there still exist areas where one is free to choose how one expends his own money. That these areas are being rapidly narrowed is self-evident. In view of the fact that FEE is attempting to widen the areas where one is free to choose, we cannot consistently complain when someone chooses not to support our work.[73]

The FEE team members were not starting out with a sophisticated model of how to achieve social change. A couple of the wealthier among them decided that one blockbuster book that would *really explain* what was wrong with collectivism, and what was right about freedom and free enterprise, could save America. They perhaps naively believed that it wasn't special-interest struggles or a desire for advantage at others' expense that created bigger government; if their fellow citizens and politicians just *understood* free markets, then public policy would embrace them. But Read and the FEE team well understood that they had a hard row to hoe, with most intellectuals and publicists spouting thirdhand Karl Marx and John Maynard Keynes. (Beginning in the 1960s, a group of economists known as the public choice school—James M. Buchanan and Gordon Tullock most prominent among them—helped fill the analytical gap that likely led Read and his colleagues to underestimate the power of special-interest groups in politics. More on them later.)

When the popular success of F. A. Hayek's *Road to Serfdom* was brought up as a counterexample to that collectivist stranglehold on culture, one person in a planning meeting pointed out that *Serfdom* likely succeeded only because Henry Hazlitt, their mole in the mainstream media, wrote a positive review that appeared on the front of the *New York Times'* book review section, which influenced the wider American intelligentsia.

Distinct from other groups on what was still then thought of mostly as "the far right"—the distinction between the libertarian and merely conservative parts of the anti–New Deal coalition didn't become clarified until the mid-1950s for many—FEE would indulge in "no disparagement of persons or organizations; discussion is limited to ideas and principles.

No telling people what to do; simply present the facts and let others draw conclusions, if any, for action."[74]

They were not for politicians or out to get the commies. They were for, in Read's inspirational phrase that gave the title to his famous essay collection, "anything that's peaceful" and against price controls (including rents and wages), public housing, loyalty oaths, forced unionism and union intimidation, and conscription.[75]

Inspired by quirky Old Right journalist and memoirist Albert Jay Nock, Read conceived of his audience in those dark times for liberty as a "Remnant" too small to dominate the culture, but who could keep the ideas of liberty alive, like medieval monks preserving ancient texts, through dark times. Read would try to find his Remnant, whoever they might be, through dogged travel and speaking, generally set up for him by local donors to FEE.

Read's vision of the Remnant was not elitist. To Read, *anyone* could end up being the most important person the freedom movement could reach.

Over and over, some businessman might be dragged by a buddy to some luncheon speech at a local Kiwanis club and find that the strange ideas of this curious evangelist named Leonard Read resonated—that some at-first strange metaphor about how the dimmest light of truth would seem very bright if it appeared surrounded by utter darkness suddenly made sense—and realize this Read fellow was telling him things he hadn't realized he already believed. And then later he'd dictate a letter to that man from FEE and Leonard Read would write back.

That letter from Read would contain some new startling yet homey metaphor that made freedom make even more sense; then the new fan of FEE would order 100 copies of Henry Hazlitt's *Economics in One Lesson* and send them on to all *his* family members, business associates, and college chums. Next time Leonard Read came through town, this new fan would drag some unsuspecting soul along, and just maybe Read's persuasive magic would work on him and the whole cycle of FEE's literature and ideas spreading would be repeated. Some FEE board members ended up taking their positions roughly that way. In its first four years, FEE had mailed out over four million pieces of literature, seen its work appear in 400 newspapers, and compiled a mailing list more than 30,000 strong.[76]

Early financial backers of FEE included the Earhart Foundation, the Volker Fund, the Mott Foundation, and an obscure newspaper from south of Read's old chamber stomping grounds, the *Santa Ana Register*, later known as the *Orange County Register*. The *Register* was owned and operated by an eccentric anarchist newspaper magnate named Raymond Cyrus Hoiles, who eventually ran a minichain of mostly small dailies scattered around the Midwest and Southwest. He named the company not after himself, like a typical newspaper magnate, but after his highest value. He named it Freedom Papers, later known as Freedom Communications before it became a separate company in 2016.

Hoiles was a hardcore modern libertarian before anyone knew what one was, before Read and FEE had begun codifying the beliefs and linking their far-flung adherents into a fledgling movement. He characterized his belief as the "single standard of conduct"—government shouldn't have the power or right to do anything an individual didn't have the power or right to do. This excludes taxation, even if the government insists the services it provides are "necessary." In 1944, Hoiles published some fresh translations of Bastiat's classic works. During World War II, he was one of the very rare newspaper publishers to write energetically against the internment of Americans of Japanese descent. He wrote:

> Few, if any ever believed that evacuation of the Japanese was constitutional. It was a result of emotion and fright rather than being in harmony with the Constitution and the inherent rights that belong to all citizens. . . . [W]e should make every effort possible to correct the error as rapidly as possible. . . .

[C]onvicting people of disloyalty to our country without having specific evidence against them is too foreign to our way of life and too close akin to the kind
of government we are fighting.[77]

He wanted to end all immigration restrictions, and liked
to spend his spare time writing letters to fellow libertarians
from Read to Ludwig von Mises explaining to them that if
they gave in on the idea that government should fund schools
with taxes, they'd have given up the whole libertarian game.

Mises, in the late 1940s, often gave lectures under FEE's
auspices. In 1948, he began his second series of lauded seminars, this time at New York University (NYU). Instead of
starring the cream of Austrian intelligentsia, it was largely
composed of young business students looking for an easy A or
B, as Mises was a notoriously kindly grader.

This seminar ensured that the Austrian economics tradition
survived in America via the small group of genuinely interested
students, who weren't always, or even mostly, seeking a degree
at NYU. As a sign of the low regard in which Mises was held
in American academia, as of 1949 his salary was paid not by
the university, but mostly by the sole libertarian funding foundation in existence at the time, the Volker Fund, and later by
some other libertarian funders recruited by Read and Hazlitt.

5

The Volker Fund

The major financier of libertarian causes and supporter of libertarian academics of the time was an obscure, long-forgotten charitable organization called the Volker Fund. The fund spent about $1 million a year to search out and support carriers of the individualist flame.[78]

One of its more important expenses was sending a squad of American economists and popularizers of libertarianism to the first meeting of F. A. Hayek's Mont Pelerin Society (more on that later).

The Volker Fund—through the conferences it sponsored, the books it arranged to be published and distributed to libraries, and its efforts to connect and build a network among scattered devotees of a hated philosophy—gave the burgeoning movement self-consciousness and intellectual depth. Volker helped find the few far-flung libertarians, bring them together, and make sure they got to work where they'd be most useful.

Volker's tactics were informed by Hayek's essay "The Intellectuals and Socialism," in which Hayek pointed out that despite socialist rhetoric to the contrary, socialism did not arise from an aggrieved working class defending its interests. People he identified as the "secondhand dealers in ideas" dictated ideology to the masses by controlling the facts, ideas, and emphases that they got from information sources ranging from university professors to the daily newspaper, a culture-wide process that was in effect "almost automatic and irresistible."[79] And that ideological class in the 1940s, not through "evil intentions" but through "honest convictions," was socialistic.[80] It was Volker's aim, by finding and helping mostly academic authors and researchers, to change that reality.

Unlike most charitable foundations, people didn't tend to come to Volker looking for support—libertarian views were so rare at the time that the fund had to actively search for thinkers worthy of its support. Volker helped keep libertarians such as Murray Rothbard and Rose Wilder Lane afloat with paying gigs reading books and journals, searching for such intellectuals.

Some academics Volker approached wanted nothing to do with the despised philosophy the fund was seen to represent, but, as Volker employee Richard Cornuelle recalled, "More common was tearful recognition that there *was* someone else out there [who believed in libertarianism]—everyone thought they were the last one."[81]

The fund was prescient when it came to economics, where libertarian ideas have had their greatest influence. Among the intellectuals Volker supported and could rely on to appear at its sponsored conferences were six future Nobel laureates in economics—Hayek, Milton Friedman, James M. Buchanan, Ronald Coase, George Stigler, and Gary Becker. Volker support was responsible for the launch of the field of law and economics, one of the most intellectually rich, though often controversial, areas of economics (Coase's work in that area won him his 1991 Nobel Prize in Economics). Friedman's brother-in-law Aaron Director received Volker funding to launch the *Journal of Law and Economics*, the first academic journal in that field, in 1958.

But in the late 1940s, Mises's star was so low because of his libertarian ideology that "we felt lucky to find some place that would take him," the Volker Fund's Cornuelle recalled. "It was more than contempt they felt for Mises. They thought he was dangerous. They thought he was pushing a vicious, inhuman position that appealed to capitalists but didn't deserve any encouragement."[82]

As Robert Nozick, Harvard philosopher and author of the highly influential 1970s libertarian political philosophy masterpiece *Anarchy, State, and Utopia*, said: "In 18 years of teaching at Princeton and Harvard, I never encountered any professor teaching a seminar where non-degree-seeking adults would continue to attend year after year. . . . [Mises was] unique in attracting mature minds without demanding discipleship." What attracted them, said Nozick, was "the content of his ideas and their power and lucidity."[83]

6

The Mont Pelerin Society

Ludwig von Mises's protégé F. A. Hayek also ended up in America, also with his salary subsidized by the Volker Fund. But before then, as World War II ended, Hayek wanted to reintegrate German intellectuals into Western culture and place his beloved lost liberalism back at that culture's center. Toward that end, he created an international and interdisciplinary society of scholars who promoted liberty and individualism. The group adopted the name Mont Pelerin Society, after the Swiss resort where it first met.

In the wake of *The Road to Serfdom*, Hayek's star was high in the scattered community of intellectuals and organizers who still believed in classical liberal ideas. On Hayek's urging, a Swiss businessman named Albert Hunold funded most of the first Mont Pelerin conference, and the Volker Fund paid for many Americans' travel to the meeting, including Milton Friedman, Aaron Director, Henry Hazlitt, F. A. "Baldy" Harper, Chicago School of economics founder Frank Knight, Felix Morley (founding editor of the journal *Human Events*), and Leonard Read.

The first meeting of Hayek's new society happened over 10 days in April 1947. The society's statement of principles decried how "the position of the individual and the voluntary group are progressively undermined by extensions of arbitrary power." They pledged allegiance to no "meticulous and hampering orthodoxy . . . with no particular party." The scattered, mostly European, intellectuals of a liberal (though in many cases not strongly libertarian) bent contributed to and attended panels on liberalism and Christianity, the future of Germany and a possible European federation, wage policy and unions, agricultural policy, and government attempts to alleviate poverty and manipulate the economy to counter business cycles.

The presence of Read and some of his FEE associates drew an important distinction between the American radical libertarians and the merely classical liberal Europeans. Europeans such as Wilhelm Röpke, Maurice Allais, and William Rappard believed in some government actions, though not total central planning, to deal with socioeconomic problems, such as poverty and unemployment. To Read, the common-sense American businessman who saw libertarianism's truths simply and starkly, these European professors didn't deserve to be considered part of an international freedom movement.[84] The European members were able to see themselves as good liberals, Read believed, just because they were slightly more freedom-minded than the collectivists and socialists who surrounded them in Europe.

Two Mont Pelerin members, Ludwig Erhard and Walter Eucken, achieved in Germany real victories for free markets. Erhard was chief economic administrator for the Allied occupation zones in postwar Germany, and he jammed through free-market policies, including freeing up prices, that helped create a postwar German "economic miracle."[85] Many of his colleagues who were helping manage the German economy also belonged to Mont Pelerin.

Unlike Read, Hayek thought a perfect Pelerine should not only believe in classical liberalism but also temper his liberalism with a deep understanding of the strongest objections of nonliberals. Milton Friedman famously told a story of Mises storming out of a room of his fellow Pelerines, condemning them as "all a bunch of socialists."[86]

One measure of the society's (or rather the society's members', since—unlike newer libertarian organizations that stake out specific public policy positions—institutionally the society does nothing but host meetings where papers are presented) success in making respectable a revived liberal ideology and scholarship is that the first meeting was attended by four future Nobel laureates, all in economics.

7

Hayek at Chicago

Hayek officially left the London School of Economics at the end of 1949 and started at the University of Chicago in October 1950. His reputation in economics was at such a low ebb—due to the eclipse of his methods and theories by those of Keynes—that he was not welcome in Chicago's economics department, but instead became a scholar in its Committee on Social Thought, an interdisciplinary degree-granting program built mostly around a Great Books model. Hayek was happy there: "I had . . . become stale as an economist and felt much out of sympathy with the direction in which economics was developing."[87]

At the end of his first decade at Chicago, he produced his most extensive explanation of his political philosophy in *The Constitution of Liberty*. Hayek's defense of liberty

is instrumental; like most from the original Austrian economics tradition, he didn't require natural rights to reach
libertarian conclusions. As he admits in the introduction:

> Some readers will perhaps be disturbed by the
> impression that I do not take the value of individual
> liberty as an indisputable ethical presupposition and
> that, in trying to demonstrate its values, I am possi-
> bly making the argument in its support a matter of
> expediency. . . . [I]f we want to convince those who
> do not already share our moral suppositions, we must
> not simply take them for granted. We must show that
> liberty is not merely one particular value but that it is
> the source and condition of most moral values.[88]

This entangling of the moral and practical, or deontolog-
ical and consequentialist, threads through most libertarian
scholars and polemicists, even if they think they are firmly
on one side or the other. That is, almost all of them believe
that liberty works best, *and* that it is morally proper—because
a libertarian's sense of moral properness is often rooted in a
belief in human rights, which is in turn rooted in a vision of
what human flourishing requires, uniting what is right and
what works.

Hayek built his intellectual edifice on the irreducible fact of human ignorance. He believed that we can never be certain of the end results of our actions, and therefore our extended social order depends on following rules instead of taking the utilitarian path of trying to figure out, in every circumstance, which action will have the best results—a task Hayek considers impossible. We ought to try to follow rules even when those whom Hayek calls "constructivist rationalists"—who believe we can restructure society to our whims via the strength of our reason—would condemn our devotion to those rules as blind or dumb.

Hayek believed that such mostly liberty-respecting rules, if followed, give the best chance for true human flourishing. That flourishing will become manifested in diversity, growth, change, and progress, in both knowledge and material goods. The free market and the unhampered price system are indispensable, thought Hayek, because they alone allow dispersed knowledge to be transmitted and brought to bear to improve the world.

The "Extreme Right"

Because of the still-real association in many people's minds of a belief in free markets with the American political right or conservative movement, Hayek felt it necessary to conclude *The Constitution of Liberty* with an essay entitled "Why I Am Not a Conservative."

His fellow libertarians felt the same way. Leonard Read tried to be friendly to everyone else in what was known by many, even sometimes among themselves, as the "extreme right." But Read knew his goals were not the same as those who—following the success of books by Peter Viereck and Russell Kirk—saw themselves in the early 1950s as "the conservative movement." By 1956, Read had noticed Kirk condemning the likes of him and FEE as "ossified Benthamites" because they advocated untrammeled liberty over tradition-based order. Read also didn't care for the obsession with commie hunting and commie fighting on the part of the mass populist right of the 1950s, even if the commie hunters also—as the John Birch Society did—promoted Misesian free-market economics.

Read's explanation of his attitude toward the John Birch Society to a FEE supporter is a classic example of Leonard the humble Zen monk: the society's leader Robert W. Welch Jr., Read wrote, "sees a communist under every bed and blames our whole socialistic mess on the Moscow apparatus. . . . No doubt your friend, Read, is just as obsessed as is Bob Welch, but my obsession takes a different turn from his. I have no fear at all of the Moscow apparatus but, rather, my own mind, my own inadequacy."[89]

Indeed, foreign policy was the most obvious fault line between the part of the anti–New Deal coalition that would become right-wing conservatism, led by William F. Buckley Jr. and his magazine *National Review*, and the straight libertarianism of FEE and Murray Rothbard and the thinkers and institutions they influenced. Buckley and his crew considered Soviet communism such a threat to liberty that any effort by the United States to defeat the Soviets, including domestic repression and taxation, was worth it. The libertarians were more apt to recognize that Cold Warriorism in a nuclear age represented such a baleful threat not only to liberty, but to life itself, that it was better to concentrate on preserving American liberties and peace than to launch a dangerous, expensive, destructive crusade allegedly to liberate the world.

FEE's curious and radical politics occasionally brought highly negative press. Eleanor Roosevelt slammed FEE in her syndicated newspaper column in 1951 for calling the welfare state "communism-socialism."[90]

In 1950, a congressional committee investigating what it called lobbying by propaganda—helmed by Rep. Frank Buchanan (D-PA), a man unsympathetic to the individualist cause—called Leonard Read and FEE to the dock to uncover who was supporting these seemingly un-American ideas. Read let agents of Buchanan's Committee on the Investigation of Lobbying dig around without serving their subpoena, then decided he had failed in his duty to his board of trustees by so doing.

When Read was preparing to testify on July 18, 1950, a WOR radio newsman, rebroadcast on a national network, anticipated the committee would "rip the cover off one of the biggest and best financed pressure outfits in America. . . . Who finances these gangs of literate goons?" The broadcast named B. F. Goodrich Tires, US Steel, Sun Oil, Sears Roebuck, and Westinghouse as complicit in Leonard Read's efforts to, among other things, "save the slums for the wealthy real estate operators who thrive on human misery." The newsman also charged that FEE used techniques similar to those "that enabled Hitler and big business to seize Germany."[91]

Everyone remembers McCarthyism and the outcry it caused a few years later, when leftists were ordered to name names, but the Buchanan Committee is a little-remembered spectacle, when the avatars of supposed right-wing reaction were forced by subpoena to name names to Congress members contemptuous of Americans who thought they had the right to refuse. Demands for lists of who they gave cash to with regard to "any attempt to influence, directly or indirectly, the passage or defeat of any Federal legislation" were dispatched to 166 captains of industry, including Read's mentor William C. Mullendore of Southern California Edison.[92]

Mullendore responded angrily via telegram with his "deepest resentment and indignation at this brazen attempt at thought-control." The protection of corporate property, part of business leaders' fiduciary duty, required fighting government attempts to control, tax, or manage that property, Mullendore insisted. That included pushing back against the government's attempts to insert itself into every aspect of life and business to such an extent that it would become impossible to know what comments or actions by the company, or those it supported financially, might relate somehow to some federal legislation. Mullendore wrote:

> If the citizen's constitutional rights to petition Congress for the redress of grievances, to freely speak and freely publish arguments and facts for the purpose of influencing opinion upon public issues is to be subjected to harassing and burdensome inquiry, and detailed, itemized accounting as to costs and expenditures, then these rights will be in the process of extinguishment.[93]

The Movement at the End of the 1950s

Such conflicts only helped highlight the vital importance of the task facing 1950s libertarians. The libertarian movement, in the first decade of FEE's existence, was in a way more like a gang than a movement—its activists, journalists, propagandists, and major funders numbered fewer than 100. (The audience for their work was in at least the tens of thousands.) They were all aware of each other, and most corresponded with one another. Discovering more fellow libertarians was an intellectual adventure and, for the Volker Fund, an expensive endeavor.

By the mid-1950s, FEE began a new version of an individualist journal called *The Freeman*, which had been edited by Hazlitt under a previous publisher. Read—who first started a for-profit company named Irvington Press to publish it before folding it into the nonprofit FEE—named as *The Freeman*'s new editor one Frank Chodorov, an unreconstructed individualist who had arisen from the Henry George movement (a libertarianish early 20th-century movement that believed the only legitimate tax was on the "unimproved value of land") and had edited a small late-1940s journal called *analysis* (Chodorov intentionally made the title lowercase). It was the first journal to publish a young economist named Murray Rothbard.

Chodorov's *analysis* embodied and continued in the spirit of Rose Wilder Lane and Isabel Paterson, publishing boldly anti-state articles that argued, for example, that "universal suffrage and representative government obscure but do not mutate the character of politics," which is to "loot without ritual."[94]

After Chodorov ceased editing *The Freeman* in 1955, it mostly eschewed contemporary politics and fell into the classic FEE style of quiet, nonconfrontational expositions of the core principles of liberty. As FEE gave *The Freeman* away for decades to anyone who asked, it served for a long period as many young libertarians' (and many young free-market conservatives'—Ronald Reagan was famously a fan) first exposure to the ideas of liberty.

While Leonard Read was, in some ways, the manager of the nascent libertarian movement in the 1950s—though not its intellectual motor; that was still mostly Mises and Hayek—he harbored his own peculiarity in libertarian terms, in that he still believed in government. Read was disturbed by how many of his compatriots thought there was no need for government at all. That attitude prevailed across the libertarian movement at the time, from Read's own employee, a former Cornell economist named F. A. "Baldy" Harper, to *Santa Ana Register* editor Raymond Cyrus Hoiles, to Rose Wilder Lane, to most of the folk running the Volker Fund, to a curious former leader in the cult of the "Mighty I Am" named Robert LeFevre, who would soon launch the first full-fledged libertarian school out in Colorado: the Freedom School. They didn't tend to use the term "anarchist"—it had connotations of terror and chaos—but that is what they mostly were. Read was not, and he feuded with many of them on the matter after writing a 1954 pamphlet specifically designed to *defend* government, "Government: An Ideal Concept."

The anarchistic thinkers around Read were not yet ready or able to systematize their anti-government philosophy. The man who would do the systematizing was already among them in the 1950s, though not yet widely published: Murray Rothbard, conceptualizer and promoter of "anarcho-capitalism."

9

Murray Rothbard

Rothbard's stated goal was to create a "thorough and systematic theory of liberty."[95] He grabbed elements from other libertarian thinkers—such as Mises's Austrian economics and a natural-rights ethic he learned from Ayn Rand. He also studied history looking for libertarian insights—such as the bloody history of state warfare and the continuous alliance between the state and big business. He was unique among the major libertarian intellectual figures in building institutions and even fighting in the trenches of electoral politics.

Murray Newton Rothbard was born in the Bronx on March 2, 1926, and grew up in New York City. He learned from Old Right newspapers such as the *New York Sun* and the *Chicago Tribune*, which was then under the tutelage of Robert R. McCormick. Rothbard in the mid-1940s thought of his philosophy as "true liberalism" and still believed that certain parts of the Republican Party stood for it. Rothbard, who became a paladin of the third generation of American adherents of the Austrian economics school, was introduced to FEE by Chicago School economist George Stigler, then teaching at Columbia University, where Rothbard attended.

Rothbard began reading the foundation's material and spending time at its headquarters, and between that and Frank Chodorov's *analysis*, realized that his true intellectual tradition was wider—and wilder—than that of the Republican Party.

Rothbard recalled arguing for his free-market radicalism sometime in the late 1940s. Someone asked him: if a social contract can justify a minimal state, then "why can't society also agree to have a government build steel mills and have price controls and whatever?" Rothbard's reaction: "At that point I realized that the laissez-faire position is terribly inconsistent, and I either had to go on to anarchism or become a statist. Of course for me there was only one choice: that's to go on to anarchism."[96]

He spent the winter of 1949 delving into the writings of 19th-century anarcho-forefathers, mostly forgotten American individualist anarchists such as Lysander Spooner (author of *No Treason*, a classic anarchist tract that demolished any argument that the Constitution represents a legitimate social contract anyone is required to obey); Benjamin Tucker (editor of the 19th century's most prominent individualist anarchist journal, *Liberty*); and Auberon Herbert (a Herbert Spencer protégé who called his anarchism "voluntarism"). Rothbard was discovering Mises's *Human Action* around the same time. His destiny was settled:

> In the fall of 1949 I was a free-market minarchist of no particular school of thought; by the spring of 1950 I was a hard-core Misesian and anarcho-capitalist, as well as an "isolationist."[97]

Rothbard wanted to use his multidisciplinary fascination with libertarian ideas to develop a unified "science of liberty." By the start of 1954, he was telling Richard Cornuelle at the Volker Fund of the glories of "a comprehensive science which rests on many foundations: praxeology, economic history, philosophy (especially ethics and epistemology)," and even "psychology, biology."[98]

Reading the correspondence of these early libertarians in the 1950s, one sees a tendency so rare and so beleaguered that even finding bright high school students who embraced libertarianism was a victory worth crowing about.

Rothbard and his young friends—including budding historian Ralph Raico, later libertarian institution builder Leonard Liggio, and economist George Reisman—formed a self-conscious intellectual and activist salon.

They called their group the Circle Bastiat, to show their continuity with the 19th-century classical liberal tradition. The group composed rousing tongue-in-cheek battle tunes, including this one, to the tune of "America the Beautiful":

It's ours to right the great wrong done, ten thousand years ago. / The state, conceived in blood and hate, remains our only foe. / O, Circle Brothers, Circle Brothers, victory is nigh. / Come meet your fate, destroy the state, and raise the banner high.[99]

The Circle Bastiat boys were also pranksters who enjoyed shaking other people's realities in a series of attempts to deliver libertarian Zen wisdom. One of their favorite stunts involved attending as a gang a talk by New Jersey governor Robert B. Meyner that was being aired on TV, and hitting him from all sides with questions that implied that *their* ideas were normal and obvious and *his* a perplexing aberration. "What, governor? You are *for* public schools? Where did you get such strange ideas? Can you recommend any books on this subject?"[100]

10

Milton Friedman

A very different strain of libertarianism from Rothbard's pugnacious system-building and cadre-building anarchism also arose in the 1950s from University of Chicago economist Milton Friedman, who wrote a pamphlet against rent control for FEE in its first year. He was also one of the small group of economists sent by the Volker Fund to the Mont Pelerin Society's first meeting.

Milton Friedman is already, and likely will continue to be, recognized as one of the most important intellectuals of the 20th century. He too saw himself as a classical liberal, an advocate of individual autonomy above the perquisites of states, unions, guilds, or church. He was aware that view made him what would now be called a "libertarian," *not* a conservative, though his intellectual success made conservatives want to claim him as their own.

For decades, Friedman was a much sought-after adviser for presidents and potentates around the world; he is significantly responsible for some major elements of the modern world, from America's volunteer army to its income tax withholding system; from floating exchange rates to a Federal Reserve that (at least for a while) held back monetary growth to curb inflation.

Friedman was born in Brooklyn on July 31, 1912, to two Jewish immigrants from Carpathian Ruthenia. Both his parents worked as dry goods merchants when they moved to Rahway, New Jersey, shortly after young Milton was born.

He attended Rutgers University, and initially intended to pursue a degree in mathematics or to become an actuary. Two of his professors, though, sparked in him a passion for economics: Arthur F. Burns (later chair of Friedman's bête noire, the Federal Reserve, and who also served on Murray Rothbard's doctoral dissertation committee) and Homer Jones, who was pursuing a doctorate at the University of Chicago while teaching at Rutgers.

Jones helped Friedman get a graduate scholarship to the University of Chicago to study economics, diverting Friedman from a scholarship offer from Brown in mathematics.

Inspired by his belief that economics was key to solving the problems of the ongoing Depression, Friedman made a choice that shaped his career and intellectual development moving forward, as he was henceforth intertwined with the University of Chicago and the intellectual tradition it represented for him and his group of colleagues and friends. Friedman and the Chicago School were rooted in the modern, mathematical, often empirical, equilibrium-model world of standard economics in a way that Mises and Rothbard and other self-conscious "Austrians" were not. Those of the Mises and Rothbard school were always suspicious of Friedman over these methodological differences.

During World War II, Friedman worked in the US Treasury's tax research division, and was partially responsible for a policy many libertarians—including his own wife, born Rose Director, whom he met and married at the University of Chicago—fault him for: the system of income tax withholding direct from paychecks. "I was one of the very small technical group that worked on developing it. . . . We were paying almost no attention to the postwar consequences of anything we did," Friedman admitted in the 1990s. "We were just asking ourselves: What can we do to win the war? I have no apologies for it, but I really wish we hadn't found it necessary to do that and I wish there were some way of abolishing withholding now."[101]

Friedman began teaching at Chicago in 1946 and remained there, with occasional years guesting at other universities, until his 1976 retirement.[102] In 1950, he launched a side career as an adviser—sometimes formal, sometimes informal—to governments across the globe, when former students invited him to work with a Marshall Plan agency.[103] While there, he proposed that Germany float its exchange rate, another cause Friedman was famously associated with, and one where his once-fantasy proposal became reality in 1973.[104] ("Floating exchange rates" means applying free-market logic about price controls to exchange rates between currencies—that governments should allow the conversion rates between currencies to be set by supply and demand, not government controls.)

Friedman's first major contribution to popular libertarianism was his 1962 book *Capitalism and Freedom*. Friedman had been a regular at Volker Fund–sponsored conferences in the 1950s, and *Capitalism and Freedom* resulted from his wife, Rose, helping him turn his speaking notes from those presentations into a book.

The book is a calm assessment of how, where, and why government fails and why private markets are both morally and practically better. Friedman traces its roots to his exposure to the intellectual give-and-take and sense of supportive community of the international world of libertarian scholars and advocates at Mont Pelerin. Friedman also credits the students who gathered around Hayek during his stint at Chicago's Committee on Social Thought during the 1950s and 1960s for creating a pleasingly libertarian atmosphere around Chicago. This group, which included Circle Bastiat mainstays Ralph Raico and Ronald Hamowy, published the *New Individualist Review*, an early and respected libertarian college magazine, for which Friedman served as an adviser.

Capitalism and Freedom was published by the University of Chicago Press. It is still in print, has sold over a half-million copies, has been translated into 18 languages, and was a favorite forbidden samizdat publication in the Soviet Union. It was a great teacher and a great symbol of respectability to young libertarians coming of age in the 1960s.

Friedman didn't rigorously establish philosophic principles from the ground up. As he put it in a 1995 interview, "I thought I was going back to some fundamentals rather than creating anything new."[105] He assumed people of goodwill all wanted prosperity and peace and explained why freedom would lead to those things, with maximum possible efficiency. He believed that arguments among economists were usually not about values, but about policies' actual or predictable effects.

Capitalism and Freedom contains, in concise form, almost all the public policy ideas for which Friedman would advocate throughout his career as a columnist, author, and speaker. Friedman grants the government should take responsibility for more than the two functions libertarians traditionally assigned to it—defense and domestic peace—protecting citizens from enemies internal and external. He also thinks government properly has power to enforce contracts, "foster competitive markets," and "enable us at times to accomplish jointly what we would find it more difficult or expensive to accomplish severally." (He grants these expansions of government responsibility can be fraught with danger to liberty.)[106]

In *Capitalism and Freedom*, Friedman delivers argument after argument that have become standard for later generations of free-market advocates, from op-ed pages to talk radio and TV. Friedman lists government functions and programs he thinks have no good reason to exist (all but the first have survived): the draft, price supports, tariffs, occupational licensing, Social Security, housing subsidies, the minimum wage, national parks, and the post office. The draft, which has disappeared (though draft registration still exists), was a particular focus of Friedman's, and he played a vital role during the Nixon administration in ending it; it's the policy victory he was most proud of (more on that later).

The book also takes swings at the basic tenets of Keynes-ianism, debunking Keynes's notion of the magic multiplier, which allegedly makes government spending better for the economy than private spending, and floats the then-unknown but now-popular idea of funding schools through vouch-ers rather than having government directly run them. He accepts the idea that government should guarantee a min-imum income for citizens, but would prefer a "negative income tax"—a direct cash payment for citizens to spend as they pleased in a free market—to replace all current social welfare programs; he argued that would be the least bureau-cratic and most economically efficient way to help the poor. This idea became part of the policy debate over how best to fight poverty before the 1960s ended, and still underlies the current debate over "universal basic income," another sign of Friedman's influence beyond the libertarian movement.

11

Barry Goldwater

Friedman's respectability and prominence earned him a spot as an economic adviser to the 1964 Republican presidential candidate Barry Goldwater. Though Goldwater was neither a part of the libertarian movement nor a consistent believer in limited government, his winning the party's nomination against great odds was nonetheless a strong tonic for the modern libertarian movement, an event that generated new energy and new recruits for a political tendency more radical than the Arizona senator himself. Almost every future libertarian movement activist, if they were between the ages of 10 and 20 in 1964, was thrilled by the image of the radical outsider Goldwater. His inspiring talk about how he came to Washington not to make laws but to repeal them helped many young libertarians see a place for themselves in the real political world.

Some were so dazzled they saw him as the living embodiment of Randian man, John Galt in a fighter plane; Rand herself was even a measured supporter. Samuel H. Husbands Jr.—a San Francisco investment professional who was on the board of directors of FEE and later the Cato Institute—thought a Goldwater victory would represent a victory for FEE's professed values; another FEE supporter told Leonard Read that Read's work in spreading the freedom philosophy was the ideological bedrock underneath Goldwater's winning the Republican nomination.[107]

Friedman's connection to Goldwater brought public attention that led Friedman to gain his most prominent polemical position: his triweekly column in *Newsweek*, beginning in 1966, where, for nearly 20 years, he explained libertarian ideas on matters both economic and personal to their largest audience to date.

Benjamin A. Rogge, a libertarian economics professor at Wabash College (and Read's choice to succeed him at FEE, though Read outlived Rogge), noted, "Goldwater's campaign could not build on any solid foundation of widely accepted ideas on society, economics, and the state."[108] If Leonard Read had taught libertarians anything, it was that mass ideological change had to come before political change, and indeed Goldwater suffered a historic drubbing against Democratic incumbent Lyndon B. Johnson.

Former *National Review* writer Garry Wills analyzed the connection between the Goldwaterite right and the libertarians: "The logistics of competition within the two-party system made Friedman, in his effort to defend Market fundamentalism, ally himself with the mishmash of Right-Wing forces behind Barry Goldwater in 1964. This was an alliance that had no true theoretical bond at all."[109] The libertarians needed the Republicans to have any nexus with the world of effective politics. What the Republicans needed from the libertarians was the only respectable intellectual theory the right had to call on: free-market economics.

"Other components of Right-Wing theory," Wills wrote, "were often mere instincts, prejudices, unformulated preferences. Only the economists marinated a respectable academic base and an intellectual tradition of any rigor."[110] Much of what interesting theory the right possesses—and it nearly always *remains* theory in Republican practice—is taken from free-market libertarianism.

12

Atlas Shrugged *and the Objectivist Movement*

Ayn Rand was still doing important libertarian work outside the realm of politics and politicians. She spent much of the second half of the 1940s working in Hollywood, fighting quixotic battles for individualist principles there, while working on her magnum opus, *Atlas Shrugged* (1957), a wild dramatization of the real-world effects of abstract philosophic principles, a tour de force that inspired life-changing awe *and* deep repugnance.

Atlas tells the story of a genius named John Galt, harmed and outraged by a foolish experiment in collective worker ownership of a factory. A world philosophically corrupt enough to accept communism does not deserve to profit from his genius, he decides. He withdraws his skills and efforts from society, and he secretly encourages other men of ability—the philosophers and industrialists and artists and financiers who do the vital tasks that keep the masses alive and thriving—to join him in refusing to contribute their values to a corrupt culture. Galt leads the first strike of the men of the mind.

As Rand portrays it, civilization collapses into misery without their genius. Then, the Great Men return from their hidden-valley individualist paradise and begin civilization over, built on Rand's own principles of Aristotelian logic, reason-based epistemology, individualist ethics, and laissez faire capitalism.

Rand detailed in *Atlas* the philosophy that would come to be known as Objectivism, especially in the 57-page speech that Galt gave over government radio waves to explain to people living in a world in ruins how their bad ideas and poor thinking were to blame for their plight. We see in the novel her philosophy providing mankind with success—grand achievements, fellowship, prosperity, and peace—while her opponents' beliefs are dramatically shown resulting in inevitable corruption, failure, self-hatred, and ultimately destruction and death.

Rand's second career as philosopher activist would likely never have happened but for her meeting and befriending young fans Nathan Blumenthal and Barbara Weidman during the writing of *Atlas*. They would later marry and become known as Nathaniel and Barbara Branden. Their energy, encouragement, and organizational skills turned Rand from just a novelist with peculiar beliefs into the driving force of a philosophical and political movement. They became her closest friends and the nexus of a small group of dedicated disciples that included future Federal Reserve chair Alan Greenspan and, for a brief time in the mid-1950s, Murray Rothbard and his young friends.

Atlas was an enormously popular success and it is still in print and selling hundreds of thousands of copies a year nearly 70 years later. However, Rand's insistence that her philosophical enemies were death worshipers, and sniveling and weak ones at that, did not endear her to the dominant forces in intellectual culture, who responded to her work with contempt. Rand did not find the great men of the world flocking to her side as she hoped. So she beat an emotional retreat.

But Nathaniel Branden knew the world needed Rand's philosophy. Though unnamed in *Atlas* itself, it became known as Objectivism. The name, Branden writes, "was applicable to her theory of existence, of knowledge, and of values. In metaphysics, she held that reality is objective and absolute, existing independently of anyone's consciousness, perceptions, beliefs, wishes, hopes or fears—that that which is, is what it is; that 'existence is identity'; that A is A. In epistemology, she held that man's mind is competent to achieve objectively valid knowledge of that which exists. And in ethics, she held that values appropriate to human beings are objectively demonstrable—in other words, that a rational code of morality is possible."[111]

Branden launched a lecture series in 1958 explaining Objectivism, which by 1961 had become the Nathaniel Branden Institute, spreading Rand's beliefs through the *Objectivist Newsletter* and lectures and recordings of lectures by her, Branden, and other trusted associates. Branden turned the novelist into the leader of a movement. She issued a series of nonfiction essay collections on her philosophy throughout the 1960s, including *Capitalism: The Unknown Ideal* and *The Virtue of Selfishness.*

By the end of 1965, taped versions of the lectures were being given in 80 cities in North America, and many outside it, with 5,000 students a year taking the courses. The *Objectivist Newsletter* evolved into a digest-sized magazine called *The Objectivist*, which by 1967 had a circulation of 21,000. Rand became a mass public phenomenon, particularly on college campuses, where in the 1960s her novels were as much a part of the intellectual landscape as J. R. R. Tolkien, J. D. Salinger, or Kurt Vonnegut, though probably because of her libertarianism, she is rarely mentioned alongside them in 1960s nostalgia.

Branden wrote in his 1989 memoir—in which he admitted that Rand's all-encompassing vision of morals and aesthetics and strong demand for personal loyalty created a cultish atmosphere around Objectivism—of the "implicit premises" of Rand's inner circle, which they tried to transmit to the students. These included that "Ayn Rand, by virtue of her philosophical genius, is the supreme arbiter in any issue pertaining to what is rational, moral, or appropriate to man's life on earth" and that "once one is acquainted with Ayn Rand and/or her work, the measure of one's virtue is intrinsically tied to the position one takes regarding her and/or it."[112]

Branden and Rand had begun an affair in the 1950s, with the knowledge of their spouses. The Objectivist theory of romantic love dictated that two people who embodied each other's highest values as those two did ought to be in love, regardless of previous attachments. Branden eventually broke off the affair and began a sexual relationship with a younger woman in Objectivist circles, a relationship he hid from Rand. When she found out what was going on in 1968, Rand broke with him in fury and shut down the Nathaniel Branden Institute. Branden went on to write a series of successful Objectivist-inspired pop psychology books on self-esteem, whereas Rand largely retreated from engagement with the world, never finishing another novel and letting her publications program peter out.

13

The Institute for Humane Studies

While the Nathaniel Branden Institute was growing Objectivism into a small but expanding popular movement in the early 1960s, F. A. "Baldy" Harper—who had left FEE for the Volker Fund in the late 1950s and was one of the few men in the libertarian movement about whom almost no one seemed to have a bad word to say—decided that the movement needed an institute to, if not *organize* libertarian progress, at least guide it. Read and FEE had gotten stagnant, in his estimation.

By 1961, Harper convinced Harold Luhnow, chief of the Volker Fund, to finance his dream: a libertarian academy, modeled after Princeton's Institute for Advanced Study, where hardcore libertarian scholars could delve into high-level, deep research on the principles of liberty and how to apply them to the real world—free of academic worries about faculty politics, teaching loads, or publishing schedules. They could thus have a better chance of solving hard problems and inventing new arguments, extending the science of liberty. Murray Rothbard and Leonard Liggio—who could have used such an institute to support their research—had brainstormed the project with Harper. Harper called it the Institute for Humane Studies (IHS).

Harper called a meeting of libertarian luminaries to hash out what the IHS could and should do. Hayek was a first among equals, as he would have been at any such gathering. He doubted that aiming the institute's efforts at students was the best use of its resources. Conservative student groups—such as Frank Chodorov's Intercollegiate Society of Individualists (later taken over by right-wingers who mistrusted individualism and renamed the Intercollegiate Studies Institute) and the William F. Buckley Jr.–inspired Young Americans for Freedom—were growing on college campuses across America by the early 1960s, but Hayek didn't think they did particularly useful work.

Libertarian arguments were not yet well developed enough to convert top-level intellectuals, Hayek insisted; therefore, to be truly valuable an organization such as IHS must strive to advance libertarian ideas on deeper, more profound levels. Free-market economics was not enough; arguments relying on philosophy and even psychology would be vital to a healthy libertarian movement's arsenal. And libertarians must not ignore where they differed—hashing out such differences is necessary for intellectual progress—and they must not respond to disagreements with schisms or attacks on heretics.

Hayek advised IHS to start small at first—perhaps just Harper and one other scholar. Its mission should be to support fine minds with an interest in liberty and see what spontaneously arose. Obsessing over the perfect plan for quick "success" would guarantee failure. Others present at the IHS planning meeting suggested that deeper study into the role of libertarian ideas in the law and business was sorely needed.

Just as big Volker money was about to fund Harper's IHS, Luhnow's growing eccentricities and a sense that he, a deeply religious man, was surrounded by untrustworthy irreligious people led him to abruptly dissolve all the Volker Fund's ongoing projects and close shop. Harper launched IHS on a shoestring anyway and kept it crawling along through the 1960s, with a small publishing and seminar program, mostly advancing the anarchist end of libertarian ideology.

14

Robert LeFevre, *the* Liberal Innovator, *and* Andrew Galambos

The Foundation for Economic Education continued to roll along. Volker Fund money was gone, but new flashes of activity popped up here and there in the far-flung and still mostly obscure libertarian movement. Since 1956, the peculiar Robert LeFevre was running a full-service multiweek education program in libertarian ideas out in Colorado, with lecturers who included Rose Wilder Lane, Frank Chodorov, Leonard Read, and Gordon Tullock, one of the founding fathers of the public choice school of economics (more on him later).

LeFevre also wrote editorials for one of Raymond Cyrus Hoiles's Freedom newspapers, the *Colorado Springs Gazette-Telegraph*. Although he promoted an eccentric, completely apolitical brand of libertarian anarchism that believed even *retaliatory* force was illegitimate, he attracted many captains of industry, especially the textile magnate Roger Milliken, who insisted his high-level executives attend the school. (Milliken, however, never totally imbibed all of LeFevre's lessons and later became a supporter of protectionist politicians.) Two of his most important students were the brothers Charles and David Koch, who went on to have a major impact on the movement in the 1970s and beyond. A financially damaging mudslide hit the school, which was insufficiently insured, and eventually led LeFevre to close shop in 1968.

Young, hip kids were also starting their own small-circulation handmade magazines pushing the edges of libertarianism, the most prominent called the *Liberal Innovator*. It launched in 1964 and focused on "long-range strategies for acquiring greater freedom . . . reports on experimental community development; news of private companies that provide what have traditionally been governmental services." The *Liberal Innovator* was early in promoting the idea of "enterprise zones"—areas with lower taxes or regulation than the surrounding nation or state to spur growth—and of privatizing government services from mail delivery to fire suppression. The zine also pioneered a continuing tendency in the movement toward advising and theorizing about ways not to change the government or culture, but to escape it via living on the high seas or hiding in the deep woods. One of the zine's principals, Kerry W. Thornley, intersected American 1960s culture in a weird way when he was accused by the New Orleans district attorney Jim Garrison of possible involvement in the John F. Kennedy assassination. Thornley had known and befriended Lee Harvey Oswald in the Marine Corps in the late 1950s and was so intrigued by this curious communist marine that he wrote a roman à clef about Oswald *before* Oswald became famous as the man who killed Kennedy.

Liberal Innovator founder Tom Marshall arose from the group of Southern California engineers who were mostly taught libertarianism by that rarest of creatures: someone making a profit as a market intellectual selling libertarian lectures. He was Andrew J. Galambos, an aerospace fanatic who had come to believe that only a truly free society would create the means to effectively transform humanity into a spacefaring species. He created the Free Enterprise Institute, the biggest local concentration of hardcore anarcho-libertarians the world had yet seen, drawing from a crowd with mostly science or engineering backgrounds. He taught how justice and defense could and would be delivered by private companies. His interpretational idiosyncrasy was a belief in intellectual property so stringent that one could not share any idea he received from someone else without paying for it. His most prominent student, Harry Browne, became a bestselling author in the 1970s selling books and investment newsletters about how the government was about to crash the economy with its inflationary paper currency and that you'd best stock up on canned goods and hard money, such as gold; he and other libertarian "gold bugs" were the driving force behind the once-quite-popular fad of "survivalism." Browne was also the Libertarian Party candidate for president twice, in 1996 and 2000.

15

The New Left and the Old Right

By the mid-1960s, with the Volker Fund gone, and unconvinced that the hawkish Barry Goldwater was anyone a libertarian should laud, Rothbard and Liggio looked toward the rising anti-war left as a semi–mass movement that might be amenable to libertarian ideas. They launched a libertarian journal called *Left and Right*, meant to bring together anti-war forces from the furthest reaches of the political spectrum.

In the first issue, Rothbard condemned the modern right as "the party of reaction, the party that longed to restore the hierarchy, statism, theocracy, serfdom, and class exploitation of the Old Order." He praised the New Left for "what it *doesn't* like, what it totally opposes in our present society, even if its vision of the ultimate future is a bit cloudy."[113]

In 1968, Rothbard's stature on the left rose when the leading lefty magazine *Ramparts* ran his lengthy declaration of how the Old Right was in important respects in alignment with the New Left, "Confessions of a Right-Wing Liberal":

> Twenty years ago I was an extreme right-wing Republican, a young and lone "Neanderthal" (as the liberals used to call us) who believed . . . that "Senator Taft has sold out to the socialists." Today, I am most likely to be called an extreme leftist, since I favor immediate withdrawal from Vietnam, denounce U.S. imperialism, advocate Black Power and have just joined the new Peace and Freedom Party. And yet my basic political views have not changed by a single iota in these two decades![114]

The right lost him when the Buckleyites took over, Rothbard complained: "A new, younger generation of rightists . . . thought that the real problem of the modern world was nothing so ideological as the state vs. individual liberty or government intervention vs. the free market; the real problem, they declared, was the preservation of tradition, order, Christianity and good manners against the modern sins of reason, license, atheism and boorishness."[115]

Rothbard also detected another problem with libertarians' ability to appeal to the left: "I am . . . convinced that one of the really big reasons that libertarianism is not making much headway among intellectuals is precisely this huge blindspot toward big business in which most of our libertarians indulge," Rothbard wrote to a friend. "There are many young lads of the 'New Left' . . . who are enormously susceptible to libertarian ideas, who are in reality libertarians and not socialists as most people believe, but who, not knowing economics and seeing supposed free-marketeers engaging in apologies for big business, flounder around with no sense of direction."[116]

Rothbard could even tolerate student radical attacks on property, as long as it was *government* property, which he saw as either stolen or essentially unowned and homesteadable. In early 1969, Rothbard assessed four distinct libertarian movement strategies in the pages of a small libertarian amateur publication called the *Libertarian Connection*, and found all of them lacking:

(1) Mere "educationism" of the sort that FEE had been trying for decades already;

(2) "Quick buck" thinking where libertarians, to insulate themselves from statism, merely tried to get as rich as possible (this attitude would grow into the very libertarian

hard-money/gold-bug movement that had its heyday in the 1970s and is alive today in the cryptocurrency community);

(3) "Retreatism"—creating new countries, searching for hidden places in the woods, and so forth, where libertarians could evade statism by just staying away from statists and the state, as per the *Liberal Innovator*; and

(4) Pure New Left–style cultural rebellion against the ways of a repressive statist culture, often called "living liberty."[117]

None of the four, in Rothbard's estimation, was enough. Education without activism was insufficient for political change; merely thriving personally as a libertarian didn't speed up a libertarian world; making a small space for liberty was insufficient for what ought to be a world-girdling revolution for liberty; and no amount of personal grooviness lessened the rights violations of the state writ large. Instead, Rothbard offered his own distinct approach, an inchoately sketched, fully revolutionary style with a professional cadre, working on two levels: a more public outreach–oriented organization or set of organizations and an internal pure-cadre gang honing the edges of libertarian ideology and making sure the hardcore remained hard. If groups were going to educate and agitate publicly for libertarianism, it was vital that what these professional libertarians taught remain properly libertarian.

In 1968, Rothbard also launched his own personal journal of libertarian theory and commentary on the politics of the day, the *Libertarian Forum*, which he published on and off until 1984.[118] Rothbard had an important new ally by 1969 as well: former Goldwater speechwriter Karl Hess, who had turned to hardcore anarcho-libertarianism.

Karl Hess

Karl Hess had been a professional journalist in the 1940s and 1950s. He became an obsessed anti-communist, and while working at *Newsweek* in the 1950s, indulged in such adventurism as trying to recruit the Mafia to disrupt domestic communism by hijacking Soviet payments to American Communist Party members. Fired for signing a pro–Joe McCarthy petition with his *Newsweek* credentials, he floated around the political right wing, and from a berth as public relations man for Champion Paper, whose president was a friend of Dwight D. Eisenhower's, found himself working on the Republican Party's platform in 1960 and 1964, when he also became a Goldwater speechwriter. Hess claimed to have been the only man on the team who actually believed Goldwater would win all the way to Election Day.

Like many Goldwater associates, Hess was mostly cut adrift from the Republican Party after Goldwater's crushing electoral loss. He began to believe in the value of small communities and individuals learning how to do for themselves as the only sure means of independence from huge outside forces, either governmental or corporate.

Unlike the culturally conservative Rothbard, Hess adopted not just New Left ideas but their look and style of activism. He sported a Castroesque beard and field jacket and became the favored libertarian leader for students wanting to get down with the whole groovy experiential revolution of those wild times. To many of them, reading Ludwig von Mises seemed less exciting than taunting riot cops to whack them over the head at an anti-war protest, and for those types, Hess made for an inspirational guru.

Hess's combination of left and right ideologies proved inspiring enough to make a US government informant who was sent to spy on the youth radical movement change his loyalties to the libertarian movement. Don Meinshausen, a young Republican and member of Young Americans for Freedom, had been tasked with reporting back to the House Internal Security Committee on the likes of Hess, but was instead converted to radical libertarianism by Hess. In a public testimony announcing his renunciation from spying for the state, Meinshausen wrote, "During my membership in SDS [leftist group Students for a Democratic Society] I learned of a much more dangerous organization which has seized and destroyed more lives and property than SDS ever could—I am speaking about the United States government." He said his new philosophy came not from Marx, but from "the revolutionary American tradition of liberty expressed by Jefferson, Webster, Thoreau, Josiah Warren, Benjamin Tucker, Lysander Spooner, Twain and others."[119]

In March 1969, Hess achieved a major victory for public awareness of libertarianism when *Playboy* published his long essay "The Death of Politics?" Hess's essay defined and defended anarcho-capitalism, giving that radical idea its widest public exposure yet, and explained how the death of the nation-state would speed along solutions to the dilemmas of drugs, war, monopoly, civil rights, and civil unrest.[120]

Young Americans for Freedom

Most of the quasi–mass libertarian activism in the late 1960s occurred under the aegis of Young Americans for Freedom (YAF). Though the group was dedicated to a Buckleyite sort of kill-the-commies conservatism and its origins were inspired by a very un-libertarian fight for loyalty oaths on campus, in the wake of Goldwater, the organization attracted many liberty-loving individualists, including many Randians, who were more libertarian than conservative.

YAF had a Libertarian Caucus going into its 1969 convention in St. Louis, led by Don Ernsberger from Pennsylvania, that wanted more libertarians in national positions with the organization. It also wanted YAF to endorse an end to drug prohibition and to become not merely anti-draft—which YAF was—but actively pro-draft resistance.[121]

Hess, denied an official speaking slot at the convention, gave a midnight speech in St. Louis under the Gateway Arch calling for YAFers to embrace the freedom in their name and abandon the conservatism that dominated the organization. About a quarter of the 1,200 YAF delegates marched to the arch to receive Hess's libertarian gospel. When the Libertarian Caucus tried running a slate of candidates for the national board, the national staff began purging libertarian-dominated delegations. A couple of California libertarian radicals went around the convention playing deliberate mind games, dressing and comporting themselves like hippies while being ideologically 100 percent pure free market, out-righting the righties.

Then, on the convention floor, came a symbolic gesture that many of those energized by it mark as *the* beginning of the modern libertarian movement: the burning of a facsimile draft card by a small group of libertarians. *Then* the depth of the typical YAF members' contempt and anger at radical libertarianism was revealed fully—in roars, shoving, fist waving, a rushing mass of bodies yearning to punch "lazy-fairy" noses. (Schoolyard-style, the conservative "trads" quickly adopted "lazy fairies" as their favorite insult to hurl at the libertarian radical "rads.")

The St. Louis conference's theme was "sock it to the left"; the libertarians and anarchists would have preferred "sock it to the state." Now libertarians and anarchists *were* the left in the eyes of the average YAFer. All the libertarian factions in St. Louis—the Libertarian Caucus and Anarchist Caucus and a LeFevrian California crew—exchanged contact information and committed to keeping open a dialogue. The next few years saw an explosion of new libertarian zines—such as *New Radical*, *The Abolitionist*, *The Individualist*, and *Rights by Right*—and of conferences across the country—such as the Left-Right Festival of Mind Liberation—attracting many hundreds of readers and attendees. Meanwhile, libertarian societies such as the Radical Libertarian Alliance, the Alliance for Libertarian Action, and the California Libertarian Alliance had sprouted from coast to coast.

The biggest and longest-lasting group to arise from all this post-YAF-break ferment was the Society for Individual Liberty (SIL), which started with 2,500 members and distributed tens of thousands of libertarian pamphlets across the nation's campuses over the next decade.[122]

A young, folk-singing LeFevrite named Dana Rohrabacher—one of the libertarian YAFers purged in St. Louis—said the young libertarian activists dreamed SIL would be their Students for a Democratic Society, but with correct ideas and lacking violent revolutionary madness, and would really change the world. SIL met a rising demand for student activism that rejected the failures of both the student left and right; within a year, SIL had 103 campus chapters.[123]

While quick world changing did not result from SIL, Rohrabacher enjoyed his time as a hippie troubadour touring the nation's campuses and crash pads singing anarcho-folk songs with lyrics such as: "Lots of people in this town/Trying to help us sinful folks/By outlawing everything from magazines/To telling dirty jokes/Oh, they think that they're helping people/By regulating what they do/But they're just putting people in jail/Folks like me and you."[124]

Later, Rohrabacher was known to the residents of Orange County from 1989 to 2019 as their Reaganite Republican member of Congress.

By the time the 1970s started, Rothbard was fed up with the New Left, seeing them as too flaky, too adventurist, unamenable to the live-and-let-live yet system-smashing possibilities of anarcho-capitalism based on complete respect of private property.

One of the reasons young libertarians failed to make significant inroads into larger youth radicalism in the late 1960s and early 1970s, theorized political historian Jonathan M. Schoenwald, was that the overwhelmingly white and male movement did not—from the evidence of most of its periodicals at the time—show much concern for the liberation *specifically* of blacks or women—although libertarians insist that their ideas about economic and personal freedom, if actuated, would topple all illegitimate hierarchies for everyone, blacks and women included.[125]

Publications from *Newsweek* to *The Nation* took curious notice of this new anarchist strain on the right at the start of the 1970s. Karl Hess was lengthily, and respectfully, profiled in the *New York Times*[126] and *Washington Post* Sunday magazines on the same day.[127] Two student radicals from Columbia University, Stan Lehr and Louis Rossetto, associated with the New York–area Radical Libertarian Alliance journal *The Abolitionist*, wrote a cover story for the *New York Times Magazine* in January 1971 on the rising libertarian movement, titled "The New Right

Credo: Libertarianism," with themselves photographed on the cover.[128] (One of them, Rossetto, played a major role in the 1990s personal computer and cyberspace revolution when he founded *Wired* magazine in 1993.) They managed to out-left the left by pointing out how the state, not the market, is to blame for air pollution and overuse of automobiles, and called for a return to a tort-liability system to prevent pollution, rather than the current system whereby someone can pollute as much as they want so long as the government approves.

16

For a New Liberty *and* The Machinery of Freedom

In 1973, two major works explaining and advocating a fully anarchistic libertarianism came out from major New York publishers: Murray Rothbard's *For a New Liberty* and David Friedman's *The Machinery of Freedom* (David is Milton's son).[129] Both explained—Rothbard from a more moral and Friedman from a more economic perspective—how every element of modern society, including justice and defense, ought to be and could be supplied in a free market without coercing customers or banning competitors.

Rothbard—hoping that a post-Watergate mass audience might finally be ready to turn their backs on government—didn't avoid some of the hardest questions a typical American might have about anarchy. He explained how streets and roads could, in economic and practical logic, be built, owned, and operated by private neighborhood associations (and how roads indeed had often been built with private money by non-state entities). Then, moving on to even harder issues than roads, Rothbard explained that even services everyone associates with the state such as courts and police could, and in some historical cases had been, provided by private-market actors. He credited the 19th-century Belgian economist Gustave de Molinari for being the first theoretician of how protection could be provided as a private-market service, just like any other service. He explained why he thought a world with no state but only competing private defense agencies shouldn't be expected to result in destructive warfare. Such conflict would naturally be bad for business for all concerned. Thus, it seemed more likely to his anarcho-capitalist mindset that defense agencies that indulge in rogue assaults on others without a defensive purpose would be outcompeted by more honest ones meeting actual consumer needs.

David Friedman, for his part, used Chicago School law and economics tools to explain that when governments claimed to be helping us all by crushing private business monopolies, they were not in fact helping, but were merely interfering in a free market that provided goods and services in the most efficient manner possible; that historically Standard Oil did *not* succeed by predatorially crushing competitors, and that in economic logic that sort of strategy would never work for any company of whatever size, wielding whatever alleged market power it had. He showed how society at large faces a deadweight efficiency loss when people steal—as the thief gains only what you lose, while you lose the stolen item plus what you spend trying to protect yourself against theft—and how private anarchist law should be expected to develop in a libertarian direction because unlibertarian laws are the kinds of public goods that free markets are not apt to provide, given that most people don't like being told what they may or may not do and likely don't want to spend their own money bedeviling people who are, at worst, harming only themselves.

17

The End of Conscription

Libertarians were vital in one of the grand achievements of the radical tumult of the 1960s, though they have not been widely credited for it. The end of the military draft in 1973 was the culmination of a long process whose respectable roots were with University of Chicago economists and advocates. Young libertarian Jim Powell from the *New Individualist Review* had toured the country speaking out against the draft. In December 1966, the University of Chicago hosted a four-day conference questioning conscription that featured students and policy intellectuals, including Milton Friedman and former Rand insider Martin Anderson, a Nixon economic adviser, who helped convince candidate Nixon to make draft abolition a priority for his administration. Nixon created a 15-member advisory commission—the Gates Commission—

tasked with producing a realistic plan to switch to an all-volunteer army; Friedman was a member.

After less than a year's worth of meetings and driven by Friedman's argumentative power on the economics of the issue, combined with moral force about the evil of treating young American men as essentially slaves, the commission unanimously recommended ending the draft.

Vietnam troop commander William Westmoreland gruffly announced to the commission that he did not want to command an army of *mercenaries*. Friedman replied, "Would you rather command an army of slaves?" Westmoreland was offended: "I don't like to hear our patriotic draftees referred to as slaves." Friedman hit back: "I don't like to hear our patriotic volunteers referred to as mercenaries."[130] Friedman then pointed out: if freely accepting monetary compensation for performing certain tasks makes one a mercenary, then he was a mercenary professor, and Westmoreland a mercenary general. Although Nixon agreed with the general shape of the Gates Commission's recommendations, he neither put them in place as swiftly as Friedman preferred nor increased enlisted troops' salaries as much as Friedman thought advisable.

18

The Libertarian Party

The Republican Party's attractiveness to libertarians was severely damaged in 1972, when President Richard Nixon imposed wage and price controls and completely cut the dollar from any connection to gold internationally, making it for the rest of the world just a piece of paper redeemable in nothing. (It had already been that for Americans since 1933.) These were acts of economic tyranny so sinister that they made Nixon seem as bad as the unnamed national leader in *Atlas Shrugged*.

David Nolan was certainly appalled. He was first attracted to libertarian ideas through the novels of the libertarian-leaning science fiction author Robert A. Heinlein, whose writing was a gateway drug for many young Americans in the second half of the 20th century. Nolan had been a former YAFer and was pals with the old Libertarian Caucus crew that had regrouped as the Society for Individual Liberty. Nolan remembered as early as the 1967 YAF national convention that disenchanted Objectivists and libertarians felt shut out. While the libertarian YAF members were commiserating, "someone sent around a piece of paper and said 'sign up on this list'—as far as I know it was the first comprehensive list of self-styled libertarians consciously trying to create a network of contacts." Eighty-eight people signed, according to Nolan's recollection.[131] Using that, a list of customers from a libertarian button-selling business he ran, and ads in small libertarian zines, Nolan spread the word that he wanted to start an actual Libertarian Party (LP).

The first Libertarian Party convention was held in June 1972 in Denver, with 89 delegates attending. The delegates drafted analytical philosopher John Hospers as their first presidential candidate, and a TV producer from Oregon named Tonie Nathan, who literally just showed up to cover the event, walked out of the convention as the party's vice-presidential candidate after she impressed the delegates with smart comments from the floor during debates over the platform and statement of principles.[132]

Although only on the ballot in two states, the fledgling party made history when Roger MacBride, Rose Wilder Lane's protégé and heir and a Republican elector from Virginia, voted not for the hated Nixon, but for Hospers-Nathan. Thus did Tonie Nathan become the first woman, and the first Jew, to receive an electoral vote.[133]

Attending that first LP convention was a California-based investment professional, Edward H. Crane, who had been turned on to politics by Goldwater and then progressed further into libertarianism through Ayn Rand and the Nathaniel Branden Institute lectures and subscriptions to the little libertarian zines of the day. Like Nolan, Crane had run out of hope for the Republican Party as a friend of liberty, and in 1974 he won the national chairmanship of the LP. When Crane noticed that letters from Roger MacBride, who wanted the LP's presidential nod for 1976, were on *embossed stationery*—you didn't see a lot of that among the LP's ragtag ranks—Crane thought, *this* is the caliber of candidate we need to run for president, and MacBride in 1976 got on the ballot in 32 states and won 173,000 votes.[134]

Crane later said he should have known the LP would fail as early as 1974, when the post-Watergate Federal Election Campaign Act became law.[135] The law imposed strict and narrow limits on the amount that individuals could donate to politicians, which closed off all possibility for one or a small group of very wealthy people to propel a candidate who couldn't gin up mass popularity from the start to prominence. That had been the lifeblood of such Democratic campaigns as Eugene McCarthy's or George McGovern's, who both received six-figure support from General Motors scion Stewart R. Mott.[136]

The law, Crane notes, "did exactly what it was intended to do: cement the two-party system in an impregnable fortress of cash from which no challenger could ever evict them."[137]

The LP won the attention and excitement of many libertarians after decades in which the cause it championed seemed too outré and hopeless to imagine meshing with the wheels of real politics. Since the movement's beginning, most libertarians, such as Leonard Read, F. A. "Baldy" Harper, Robert LeFevre, and even Rand, saw their mission as more for inculcating the proper moral and philosophical principles than about shifting real-world politics.

19

Samuel Edward Konkin III

Even as the LP and the notion of public policy think tanks (more on that later) first reared their heads in the movement in the 1970s, some influential libertarians saw electoral politics as a snare. Samuel Edward Konkin III, editor of the zine *New Libertarian Weekly*, called his nonpolitical variant of the movement "agorism," after the Greek word for "market." The true libertarian vanguard, he insisted, were neither politicos nor scholars nor journalists, but those actively creating institutions and markets beyond—and often hidden from—authorities and tax collectors. Black-market unregulated businesses that paid no taxes were the true vanguard of the libertarian revolution.

Konkin's ideas have remained influential, especially in the digital age, far beyond the small numbers who would ever have read his zine. Such libertarian-rooted phenomena as the dark website Silk Road—which allowed far-flung users to trade cryptocurrency for any shippable commodity, most often illegal drugs, from sellers who were community-rated (using a tightly encrypted secure web browser)—are a prime example of Konkinian agorism. (Although Silk Road was shut down by the feds, the concept has been picked up by a stream of imitators.)

Konkin promoted a more daring version of ideas that old Volker hand Richard Cornuelle had promoted in the 1960s, and aspects of the highly apolitical Robert LeFevre vision: libertarians needed to show, not tell, how markets and liberty made the world freer, richer, and more option-filled via the black market and extrapolitical actions. The Konkin vision insisted libertarians shouldn't believe they had to succeed in actually eliminating the state—or convince the masses that the state ought to be eliminated—to start "living liberty" immediately.

Some libertarians, not directly influenced by Konkin, tried to create not just free *markets* in the shadows but actual free *countries*. Such efforts included sailing home-built boats to the Bahamas, taking possession of small atolls near Fiji to dredge up some dry land, and making common cause with separatist rebels from the Bahamas to Vanuatu. None of these schemes worked, and Robert Poole—a longtime editor of the libertarian magazine *Reason* and leading American advocate of privatization—concluded, "Believing we'd be able to steal away with something that appeared to be unclaimed or engineer a libertarian revolt without massive external backing was very naive."[138] Still, similar efforts continue.[139]

20

The Koch Brothers

Such naiveté likely arose from a sense of desperation. Despite growth and enormously increased public attention since the 1950s, libertarianism was still the most underfunded and undermanned ideological tendency in America. That started to change in the mid-1970s when Charles Koch—who ran a huge privately held petrochemical firm and had attended LeFevre's Freedom School and then became board chair at the Institute for Humane Studies when Harper died in 1973— began financing a wide variety of libertarian institutions, publications, and causes.

Those included launching a new institution, along with Rothbard and the Libertarian Party's Crane, called the Cato Institute, the first real public policy "think tank" for libertarian ideas, not just about education but about proposing workable policy change to policymakers. In the late 1970s, not only this new Cato Institute but also the LP, Students for a Libertarian Society, *Inquiry* magazine (a left-outreach magazine of libertarian commentary and reporting), and *Libertarian Review* were all largely Koch-financed or hired people who were.

A certain libertarian flavor was flaring up in American politics, especially after the victory of the property tax–cutting Proposition 13 in California in 1978—a year that Edward E. Clark, running for governor and a member of the Libertarian Party, got more than 5 percent of the vote in that state. He ran for president with the LP in 1980, with Charles Koch's brother David as his running mate. Theirs remained the most effective LP campaign until 2016, earning 921,000 votes, over 1 percent of the total. The Kochs stopped dealing with the LP after their preferred candidate failed to win the nomination in 1984. Although the party hung around nominating, among others, former and subsequent Republican representative Ron Paul (1988) and best-selling investment crisis author Harry Browne (1996 and 2000), it didn't reach that same level of votes until 2012 with the former Republican governor of New Mexico, Gary Johnson. In 2016, Johnson beat all LP records by earning 4.5 million votes, 3.3 percent of the national vote, perhaps a function of the unusually large public antipathy toward both major party candidates that year.[140]

A major Koch-funded project in the 1970s was to support seminars, books, and academic programs to revive the Austrian economics tradition in America, a project that seemed more promising in the wake of Hayek's unexpectedly winning the Nobel Prize in Economics in 1974. Over the next decade or so, small centers of Austrian teaching were launched at New York University and George Mason University in the northern Virginia suburbs of Washington, DC. The "dean" of this generation of academic Austrians was Israel Kirzner, who earned his doctorate under Ludwig von Mises at NYU in the 1960s.

21

Robert Nozick

In 1975, modern libertarian political philosophy hit the big time when Harvard professor Robert Nozick's *Anarchy, State, and Utopia* won the National Book Award for Philosophy and Religion. Nozick shook up the academic world with his sophisticated arguments for libertarian political positions that most of his fellow academics found repellent. Movement libertarians were similarly impressed, if also similarly not convinced.

Nozick wrote in the introduction to *Anarchy*, "It was a long conversation about six years ago with Murray Rothbard that stimulated my interest in individualist anarchist theory."[141] Formerly a social democrat, Nozick said he "never actually encountered principled arguments for capitalism. I encountered arguments that said, well, there will be higher productivity under capitalism, which I think is true, but nothing that spoke to certain moral concerns that one might have about whether it was a legitimate system." After being introduced to Rothbard's anarchist ideas by Rothbard himself (who was introduced through a mutual friend), Nozick realized that political philosophy had a task too many of his colleagues ignored: to rigorously defend the existence of the state at all.

In doing so, Nozick didn't end up at Rothbard's anarchism, but created a complicated and nuanced defense of a state restricted in its rightful powers, which he saw as mostly just defense and adjudication of disputes. Nozick brought libertarian ideas to the center of the academic philosophical argument, and as a result "there may have been many parties I wasn't getting invited to because people despised the views in my book," he later said.[142]

Nozick presumed that in a world of private competing defense agencies à la Rothbard, one would naturally grow larger than the others through economies of scale and would trap its rivals in a vicious spiral to irrelevance. Supposing a moral principle that one can prohibit actions if they pose an undue risk to harm others, Nozick, through a complicated chain of reasoning, presumes that such an agency could prohibit the enforcement of risky adjudication standards on its clients.

Thus, through something like "market forces," an entity that is essentially a state arises—one that, however, would be obligated to compensate those who feel aggrieved by having their opposing private defense firms quashed by providing them free defense: voilà, thought Nozick, a morally tolerable state.

Although he spent a third of his book *defending* the state, he went on to drive most liberal academics crazy by then demonstrating that providing defense and justice was *all* that state could morally do, contra John Rawls's popular treatise, *A Theory of Justice*, which defended income transfers in the name of achieving greater equality.

Nozick advocated an "entitlement theory" of rights, which stated that we deserve any unowned thing we first obtain from a state of nature (as per John Locke), as well as any previously owned thing that is offered to us freely in a mutually agreed trade, or even as a gift. Even if you didn't own any private property, Nozick insisted, a world that respected property rights would be one in which any given person would likely be better off—as a look at the wealth generated by the capitalist system revealed—than in a world that tried to eliminate property rights.

Nozick concluded that his libertarian minimal state might be the closest mere humans can come to utopia—not a utopia where one single vision of the good life rules over all, but a cornucopic world where people freely choose communities to meet their unique needs without some overweening state insisting we all have to agree on what the good life is like. "Utopia is meta-utopia," he wrote, "the environment in which utopian experiments may be tried out; the environment in which people are free to do their own thing."[143] That's what libertarians had been fighting for all along.

Many libertarian academic philosophers have arisen after Nozick and independent of his influence—including Rand-influenced ones such as Tibor Machan, Douglas Den Uyl, and Douglas B. Rasmussen, and more eclectic ones such as Loren Lomasky, Jan Narveson, Michael Huemer, Jason Brennan, and Anthony de Jasay. Yet the post-Nozick political and legal philosopher who has had the most contemporary influence is from the Rothbardian tradition, Georgetown University's Randy E. Barnett.

22

Randy E. Barnett

Barnett began working with libertarian institutions during the mid-1970s in the days of the Center for Libertarian Studies. He credits scholars associated with that organization—Walter E. Grinder, Leonard Liggio, and Murray Rothbard—with keeping him in the libertarian orbit as he shifted from law student to big-city prosecutor in Chicago to law professor. In the 1990s, Barnett wrote the most convincing philosophical defense of anarchism of the decade, though he avoids the term "anarchism," choosing to refer instead to "polycentric legal systems."

Barnett eases in the doubtful slowly. He suggests two tiny restrictions: you can't force customers to pay for your services, and you can't use force to drive your competitors out of business. That sounds perfectly reasonable to most people, and would lead, Barnett thinks, to a functioning anarchism with competing legal codes and defense agencies that would meet the human need for order. Despite being a huge booster of 19th-century individual anarchist Lysander Spooner (who believed the Constitution held no authority over anybody beyond its signers), Barnett wrote a book arguing that the Constitution, properly understood, allows only laws that "are both necessary to protect the rights of others and proper insofar as they do not violate the rights of the persons whose freedom they restrict."[144] That is, Barnett believes that a properly interpreted US Constitution is a perfectly libertarian document. Even with these radical ideas, Barnett has become recognized from academia to mainstream media as one of the most influential legal thinkers and activists of our time, with key roles in the legal fights for medical marijuana, arguing before the Supreme Court in the 2004 case *Gonzales v. Raich*, and against the Obamacare individual mandate to buy health insurance under threat of financial penalty.

23

Milton Friedman, Redux

The mid-1970s saw another huge reputational leap for libertarianism when Milton Friedman won the Nobel Prize in 1976, two years after Hayek.[145] Although the award was for his technical contributions to economic sciences, he was equally a prize winner as a political advocate. He can convincingly be said to have won policy victories, from the volunteer army to floating exchange rates and the elimination of legal ceilings on interest rates.

In his *Newsweek* columns, Friedman exposed to millions of average Americans—while keeping his commentary rooted in current events—the basics of monetarism (commenting on the actions and follies of the Federal Reserve were a common theme, especially in the inflationary 1970s); the foolishness of wage and price controls; and his belief, adopted by many fiscal conservatives, that since governments will spend every penny they get their hands on via taxation plus extra, raising taxes is never an acceptable solution to deficit spending. He explained why volunteer armies and school vouchers were good and why the minimum wage, urban renewal policies, and usury laws were bad. His was the most prominent voice for free markets and individual liberty in American journalism for two decades.

In 1980, Friedman had his greatest impact as a libertarian polemicist with his book and TV series *Free to Choose*; the companion book sold over a million copies.[146] Friedman felt he should try to teach anyone who would listen about proper economic policy, which included many consultations with governments, including ones whose behavior and policies he strongly and obviously disagreed with, such as those of Yugoslavia and China. Friedman's meetings with such unlikely interlocutors accorded with his belief that libertarian ideas might win public acceptance in cases when the existing systems faced near-crisis situations, and he would speak to anybody who would listen.

But that doesn't mean those overtures weren't controversial. Because some of Chilean dictator Augusto Pinochet's advisers had attended the University of Chicago—indeed, they were internationally known as the "Chicago Boys"—and because Friedman himself had one meeting with the dictator, many people blamed Friedman and his libertarian ideas for Pinochet's tyrannies. Angry opponents of Pinochet even picketed the Nobel ceremony when Friedman won his prize. Although Friedman did approve of certain of its strictly *economic* policy choices, he had "nothing good to say about the political regime that Pinochet imposed. It was a terrible political regime."[147]

Most of the major Chicago School figures beyond Friedman did not knowingly enter the scrum of ideological activism for libertarianism or any other ideology; however, the body of arguments in favor of free markets would be far poorer without them—to name a few examples, Harold Demsetz's work on antitrust and industrial concentration, which cast doubt on the necessity of an activist government breaking up big companies; Sam Peltzman's work on the efficacy and rationality of government regulatory agencies, which cast doubt on their ability to meaningfully manage consumer safety and economic efficiency without being captured by the very forces they mean to regulate; Yale Brozen on both those issues; or Gary Becker, whose relentless application of economic thinking to all sorts of social behavior led to the conclusion that racial discrimination was economically irrational and could be expected in the long run to be competed away in a free market without the need for government intervention.

24

Israel Kirzner and the New Austrian Economists

Israel Kirzner outlined Austrian economics' differences with the neoclassical mainstream in a contribution to an early 1980s book, *The Crisis in Economic Theory*:

> Modern mainstream economics displays a number of related features which, for Austrians, appear as serious flaws. These features include especially: a) an excessive preoccupation with the state of *equilibrium*; b) an unfortunate perspective on the nature and role of *competition* in markets; c) grossly insufficient attention to the role (and subjective character) of *knowledge*, *expectations*, and *learning* in market processes; and

d) a normative approach heavily dependent on questionable *aggregation* concepts and thus insensitive to the idea of *plan coordination* among market participants. Together these flaws represent very serious distortions, at best, in the understanding of market process in capitalist economies which modern neoclassical economics is able to provide.[148]

Gerald P. O'Driscoll Jr., an Austrian economist who spent much of his career working at the Federal Reserve Bank of Dallas, insists that Austrians have kept the flame of the core insight of classical economics, best expressed by Adam Smith: that spontaneous order arises from freely acting people. Modern economics, particularly after the rise of John Maynard Keynes, often insists that some sort of government action is necessary to make markets form a tolerably workable order; Austrians, by contrast, tend to believe that a proper understanding of human action and incentives in an uncoerced market indicates that economies function best without government intervention.

However, economists, like most academics, even those in the Austrian tradition, stress that they are pursuing an economic research program to understand the world, not intended per se to support any given political position, whether libertarian or not.

Still, a link between libertarian politics and Austrian economics clearly exists. Three of the most prominent economists in the Austrian tradition of the 20th century—Mises, Hayek, and Rothbard—were also political philosophers of a libertarian or anarchist bent. Mises's economics treatise *Human Action*, the first grand treatise on all of economics in over a generation, did not make a significant splash in his academic profession, but was rather mostly read and praised by businesspeople and conservative and libertarian activists and intellectuals. With *The Road to Serfdom*, Hayek turned his efforts more to politics than economics. The Austrian economists' insights were applicable to everything from price formation to international trade. The Austrians' ability to explain how human needs tend to be met via spontaneous order, and how interfering with those orders can diminish human wealth and well-being, have long provided intellectual support for libertarians.

25

James M. Buchanan and Public Choice

In 1986, another economics Nobel went to someone from the larger libertarian world, James M. Buchanan, dean of the public choice school of economics. The Volker Fund had been an early supporter of the Thomas Jefferson Center for Studies in Political Economy and Social Philosophy, which Buchanan ran at the University of Virginia, and supported other libertarian thinkers, such as Hayek and Italian legal scholar Bruno Leoni, for half-year stints there. Buchanan explained the libertarian implications of his approach to economics this way: "The Virginia [public choice school] emphasis was, from the outset, on the limits of political process rather than on any schemes to use politics to correct for market failures."[149]

Buchanan, along with Gordon Tullock, built a rigorous scholarly apparatus and eventually a strong professional consensus around the idea that—despite what many economists with more inherent respect for government tended to assume—government agents' actions ought to be modeled the same way economists tend to model the behavior of private individuals and firms in markets. In other words, it's reasonable to expect politicians and bureaucrats to be motivated by maximizing their own utility, more than by any high-minded striving for the "public good" or "social welfare function" calculable by a technical economist. Both men ended their careers at George Mason University in Virginia, which has been a center for economic scholarship in the Austrian tradition since the 1980s; George Mason also became the home for F. A. "Baldy" Harper's Institute for Humane Studies (though long after his death) and has been the American university with likely the largest concentration of libertarian or libertarian-leaning scholars over the past few decades.

26

The Reagan Years and Fusionism

The 1980s saw the libertarian movement grow and become slightly more mainstream, building on work done by libertarian thinkers and organizations in the previous decades over a wide variety of disciplines and areas, including not just economics and academic philosophy but psychiatry and science fiction. Ronald Reagan's winning the presidency in 1980 was, in its way, a manifestation of libertarian success since, rhetorically at least, he sang a very libertarian tune—in his first inaugural address he declared that "government is not the solution to the problem, government is the problem."[150]

Ronald Reagan was famously a reader of *The Freeman*; he was photographed the day after his election examining a copy of Leonard Read's journal, with his wife Nancy's head on his shoulder. He told the libertarian magazine *Reason* in 1975, "The heart and soul of conservatism is libertarianism."[151] The economic advisers surrounding him contained various movement figures, including Milton Friedman and Ayn Rand's friend Alan Greenspan. Former Robert LeFevrite troubadour Dana Rohrabacher was one of Reagan's speechwriters.

His action failed to live up to his rhetoric, and movement libertarians were not impressed. Despite his professed love for 19th-century radical free trade heroes and proto-libertarians Frédéric Bastiat, Richard Cobden, and John Bright, Reagan raised tariffs and imposed import quotas, increased farm subsidies and quotas, and ramped up the war on drugs. His tax cuts were blunted by tax increases via "loophole closing" and inflationary bracket creep. With the advice of Rand's close associate Alan Greenspan, who also faced strong reprobation from many libertarians for abandoning Randian principles, he "saved" Social Security by raising payroll taxes. Most of the valuable deregulations of the era—air travel, freight rail, trucking—occurred during Jimmy Carter's administration, not Reagan's.

Reagan talked of abolishing useless federal agencies, but the targeted Energy and Education departments survived him and still survive.

Still, the *spirit* of the Reagan revolution was more libertarian than conservative—tax cuts and deregulation were not crusades rooted in old conservative notions of traditionalism and order. Although regulation may sound like order, it was libertarians who promoted the notion that true order was spontaneous and arose from freedom. What passed for conservative thinking was often more accurately libertarian, while organizations like the Cato Institute and Reason Foundation grew in stature, cash, and influence in the Reagan era—with far greater growth ahead.

Charles Murray

The 1980s also saw a new wave of free-market institutions that split the difference between conservatives and libertarians by stressing only their areas of overlap, many of them seeded by the Leonard Read–influenced Antony Fisher from Britain, who founded its leading free-market think tank, the Institute of Economic Affairs, in 1955. In the 1980s, he tried to essentially franchise that model, which had its strongest effect on American politics via the Manhattan Institute.

Charles Murray, writing under Manhattan's aegis, is a libertarian intellectual who had a direct and rapid effect on a vital policy debate. His 1984 book *Losing Ground* was commissioned and shepherded to completion by Joan Kennedy Taylor (a former member of Rand's inner circle and a staffer on *Libertarian Review*, whom Murray described as "the equivalent of the person discovering me sitting on the stool at Schwab's Drug Store").[152] Murray's work for the Manhattan Institute—which was run at the time by former Center for Libertarian Studies chief William M. H. Hammett—quickly dominated the welfare policy debate.

Murray argued that the late 1960s' wave of income transfer programs didn't improve the lives of the poor and even made them worse off. Trendline analyses show, he insisted, that improvement after the programs went into effect just continued progress that began before federal welfare programs, and that the progress often slowed or stopped as the welfare program's effects took hold. Crime and unemployment increased for the poor after the welfare state took hold as educational achievement and income decreased.

Murray used thought experiments to show that, because the poor respond to incentives the same as anybody else, the incentives created by the modern welfare state made it more likely that children would be born out of wedlock and that men would feel less need to work to support their children. The debate he launched was hugely influential on the 1990s' Clinton-era welfare reform debate.

The Cold War and After

In the Reagan years, a young libertarian activist became the first American to be prosecuted for refusing to register for the draft—or what remained of it. Even after the draft officially ended, *registration* for it, under the anodyne pseudonym "Selective Service," has continued, zombie-like, as a requirement for all men between 18 and 26 years old. Students for a Libertarian Society, a Koch-funded college group that thrived from 1979 to 1982, opposed that practice as one of its prime goals. But Paul Jacob—who was working for Edward E. Clark's 1980 Libertarian Party presidential campaign when registration became law again—responded with civil disobedience.

And not quietly, either. He protested publicly and advocated that others also refuse to register. When the government demanded he turn himself in, he ran off on a national campaign of libertarian activism and was eventually caught and arrested in 1984. The only people the government tried to prosecute, he pointed out, where those like him who *publicly* defied them, meaning he was being prosecuted not so much for not registering, which thousands did without facing legal consequences, but essentially for an act of free speech: condemning draft registration out loud.

Jacob had registered to vote; on his voter registration card, he had written the libertarian slogan "smash the state." A then-obscure Republican member of Congress sympathetic to libertarianism, Ron Paul from Texas, traveled on his own dime to testify on Jacob's behalf. Paul was asked to explain those inflammatory words. He said that while he might not use those exact terms, he understood the sentiment.[153] (Jacob was convicted and spent five and a half months in jail, and has worked in libertarian activism ever since.)[154]

Despite the end of the Cold War, military intervention continued to split libertarians from conservatives. During the 1991 Gulf War, which Cato scholars strongly opposed, some of Cato's funders, such as the right-wing John M. Olin Foundation, stuck with the Republican coalition on foreign policy. Olin's then president William Simon—former treasury secretary under Nixon and author of one of the huge bestsellers that marked the late 1970s as an era of popular free-market thought, *A Time for Truth*—told Cato founder Edward H. Crane, "You cannot imagine how astonished I was—indeed 'outraged' would be a better word—to read . . . your description of the recent war in the Gulf as a conflict in which 'the world's most advanced military power laid waste to a Third World nation . . .' and your lament that 'It really is a tragedy that so many good free-market conservatives have signed off on the Gulf War.'"[155] Cato lost nearly $1 million in funding over its consistently libertarian position on the war.[156]

27

Conclusion:
Recent History and
Going Forward

By the dawn of the 1990s, thanks to the often-subterranean ideological work of these libertarian thinkers and activists, the *Wall Street Journal* noted, "Because of their growing disdain for government, more and more Americans appear to be drifting—often unwittingly—toward a libertarian philosophy."[157] Famed Washington watcher E. J. Dionne was seeing libertarianism as "the *latent and unconscious* ideology of millions of new voters."[158]

Recent survey research indicates that about 14 percent of Americans hold roughly libertarian political notions. Now, they certainly haven't all been directly exposed to explicitly ideological libertarian writings, but the movement has punched above its weight in the culture so much for so long that, for a significant number of people, libertarian ideology has become the sea in which they swim. In 2008 and 2012, Ron Paul—who in 1988 ran for president as a Libertarian Party candidate and whose ideology was shaped by the Foundation for Economic Education, Mises, and Rothbard—ran a campaign focused on liberty, peace, and hard money that won 2.1 million primary votes in 2012. National youth organizations pushing libertarian ideas flourished, either as an outgrowth of that campaign directly, in the case of Young Americans for Liberty, or just in the wake of its ferment, as in the case of Students for Liberty. Once again, libertarian intellectual conferences abound across American college campuses.

Libertarian ideas in the 21st century have inspired over 20,000 Americans to commit to moving to New Hampshire (a state chosen by vote of early interested parties for, among other reasons, its already favorable political environment and its abnormally large legislature, which makes it possible to become a lawmaker with a few thousand votes) as part of the

Free State Project to try to turn that state's political culture and practice in a libertarian direction.

Bitcoin, a digital "free-market money" whose early adopters were nearly all libertarians, generated what is likely the most extreme asset value increase in human history and led to an explosion of new cryptocurrencies outside the control of any state.

Electoral politics pose a major challenge for libertarian-oriented candidates because they need to find voters who agree with a full, or nearly so, set of libertarian ideas and policies. And as we have seen in the past with Goldwater, the lapse between a candidate first arising as a radical outsider in a party to his ideas dominating it can be long. However, when taken à la carte—via legislation or (more commonly) ballot initiative—libertarian causes from school choice and home-schooling to marriage equality to marijuana decriminalization have won unprecedented victories in the 21st century.

Any libertarian momentum in the Republican Party that might have been predicted from Paul's success—or the ascension of his son Rand Paul to the Senate and to national fame for filibustering in 2013 against executive power to arbitrarily kill American citizens in the name of the war on terror—seems blunted by the election of the most anti-libertarian choice the party offered, Donald Trump.

The libertarian movement has certainly not made a libertarian America. What the government takes, what it regulates, has not shrunk significantly; the powers in foreign policy and secret investigations and arrests that the executive branch grasps only keep getting greater and more expansive.

Still, black Americans, or women, or those who like reading odd and unpopular books, or who want to marry outside their race or within their gender, might find libertarian complaints about government growth missing some very important elements. Most of them are certainly freer than they would have been in the 19th century, when government by measures of spending or taxation or regulation was "smaller," regardless of the size of their tax burden or the existence of the Jones Act (restricting shipping between US ports to US-flagged ships) or the Davis-Bacon Act (regulating wages paid to federal contractors) or the National Security Agency's domestic spying.

Some highly valued liberties flourish outside the libertarian movement's focus on the size and activities of government. Far from resisting this idea, libertarians might want to study and even take some solace from the fact that major sea changes in public attitudes related to tolerance of others' behavior can and do happen. Liberty as felt in one's individual life has components that go beyond government actions and how we might react to them.

As of this writing, a focus that recognizes the dangers of societal intolerance is coming to greater prominence in the movement, especially among younger libertarians. At the same time, that attitude has seen some pushback. A faction that took over the Libertarian Party in 2022 calling itself the "Mises Caucus" (more from the influence of the Ludwig von Mises Institute than from Ludwig von Mises's own work) was resolutely against any messaging that implied that personal tolerance, especially being openly and explicitly anti-racist, was to be encouraged in the Libertarian Party or movement. They believed that bigoted attitudes were mere "thought crimes" of no concern to libertarianism properly conceived, which in their minds must only consider actual physical attacks on person or property as worthy of condemnation.

On the other hand, some libertarians hold resolutely to the notion that theirs is a strictly political philosophy, only concerned with the uses of state force.

The movement itself—as the preceding debates show—has never been richer, healthier, or more varied. A libertarian in these early days of the 21st century can attend weekend or weeklong conferences full of libertarian speakers, lecturers, and socializing sponsored by Students for Liberty, or the Reason Foundation, or the Cato Institute, or a variety of freelance event organizers.

The web is filled with more libertarian pundits, professional and amateur, than you could read if you spent all day doing it, reaching millions of people with libertarian ideas monthly. The burgeoning world of podcasts also has room for far more libertarian voices than the old world of radio and TV ever did.

Libertarian scholars, often financed and guided through their graduate programs by the Institute for Humane Studies, can find university appointments without fear that their ideology will get them blackballed by colleagues.

Libertarian voices have included that of John Stossel, formerly of ABC News and converted to libertarianism by *Reason* magazine, who enjoyed his own cable TV show for years. Libertarian legal action group the Institute for Justice (IJ) has litigated more than 200 cases fighting government attempts to deny people employment, take their property, or quash their speech, and has won four out of the five cases it took all the way to the Supreme Court. Libertarian legal theories are gaining ground in the "conservative" legal movement and influence court decisions. Even when the IJ lost on the surface in the 2005 *Kelo v. City of New London* Supreme Court case, the injection into the public and legal debate of libertarian ideas about property rights in the context of the controversy has led to nearly every state passing some form of eminent domain reform that provides tougher hurdles for the government to jump over before taking private property for allegedly public purposes.[159]

And while the 21st-century world of social networks is a way to spread any and all ideas—from the banal to the paranoid to the bigoted—those who watch the world of libertarian discourse will see that libertarian belief in the value of free markets and deep and healthy mistrust of government actions are more than holding their own in that arena.

In the Leonard Read spirit of lighting the candle of liberty one mind at a time, the libertarian movement has done very well for itself. People by the hundreds of thousands *have* received economic education in the original spirit of FEE. They *have* learned, say, that minimum-wage laws tend to harm lower-wage workers by pricing them out of the market; that the welfare state's incentives might tend to halt self-sufficiency rather than promote it; that if trade protectionism seems to help an American business, the benefit is outweighed by the harm to all other Americans, who are paying more for less; that having poorer countries engage in less restricted international trade will enrich, not impoverish, them; that increasing inflation is not a long-term cure for unemployment;

that drug laws drive up drug prices, increase property crimes, and makes the users' problem society's problem. Rose Wilder Lane's dream for a libertarian movement in its earliest days was that "at the end of this century there will be a higher percentage of people believing in liberty than ever before."[160] And there certainly were.

The 21st century has seen technological advances and possibilities that have brought us—ever so slightly—closer to a Sam Konkin–like "agorist" world, where libertarians and nonlibertarians alike can evade government restrictions and meet market needs freely. And it has all been possible without the ideological superstructure of libertarianism, as the movement has pushed it for the past century, being adopted fully or even understood by large swaths of the public.

Indeed, since the 1990s, the technicians and businesspeople and ideologues who constitute some of the greatest wealth and option-created action in the American economy—the world around Silicon Valley and its worldwide offshoots—have begun to actualize a digital high-tech future—a world in which government has little, or no, place. In such a world, the state would just be an extraneous interference to getting interesting, wealth-creating things done. As libertarian John Perry Barlow, a lyricist for the Grateful Dead and founder of the Electronic Freedom Foundation, declared in a famous cyberworld manifesto:

> Governments of the Industrial World, you weary giants of flesh and steel, I come from Cyberspace, the new home of Mind. On behalf of the future, I ask you of the past to leave us alone. . . . You have no sovereignty where we gather. We have no elected government, nor are we likely to have one, so I address you with no greater authority than that with which liberty itself always speaks. I declare the global social space we are building to be naturally independent of the tyrannies you seek to impose on us.[161]

These all promise an increasing ineffectiveness and perhaps irrelevance for government as we have known it. The libertarian-minded in the 21st century have innovated areas from private space travel to smartphone-enabled ridesharing to homemade firearms, and find themselves butting up against government at every turn. People growing up in a world with our current technological possibilities in commerce, production, and communications might find themselves with less practical reason to believe they need big government—or any government at all.

The most extreme movement advocating a richer, freer, more powerful human future, the extropians/transhumanists, are an offshoot of the libertarian movement. Their ideas about liberated humans warping their minds and bodies through technologies of all varieties—living forever, blasting off to the stars, or downloading their minds to computers—were presaged in the 1970s' writings of the libertarian former acid guru Timothy Leary. Leonard Read used to define the libertarian message as "anything that's peaceful." Modern libertarians of extropian-transhumanist leanings (who are still a minority even among libertarians) have extended that to *everything* that's peaceful—whatever notion humanity can get the technology to achieve, let's go for it, let's—like our classical liberal forebears Wilhelm von Humboldt and John Stuart Mill—celebrate the wild abundance of experiments in living that a liberated human being might choose.

Aware, self-conscious libertarians, and libertarian ideas in general, are still a minority in America today. The political scene of the past decade is not particularly encouraging for them, with both major parties pushing some variety of national and worldwide economic management, taxing and spending now, or borrowing to cover the spending now and pushing off the taxing to a later generation to keep the government solvent. Various crises, both fiscal and monetary, that libertarians have warned about still loom on ever-nearer horizons. Although some elements of the Republican Party have learned the lessons of the Iraq War at the turn of the 21st century when it comes to full-on boots-on-the-ground war making to shape foreign nations' politics, the safety (for the operator) of drone warfare has meant that there has been little meaningful clawing back of America's expensive, enemy-making overseas adventurism.

And some segments of American political culture in the past decade or so have shown a greater tendency toward a near-violent intolerance of certain differences or certain peoples, and a sense that our political dilemmas or our political opponents themselves might need to be dealt with violently rather than through the peaceful changing of minds.

But none of the thinkers or institutions that have shaped or constituted the American libertarian movement over the past century promised a quick victory. They merely asserted that an understanding of political philosophy, human nature, ethics, and economics dovetailed with a belief that free human beings are apt to deliver the richest and most varied world it is possible for humans to build, and that the spirit of government, of control, of interference in peaceful free choices, was ultimately a weight holding back human progress, both moral and economic. They understood that a combination of human factors, from economic misunderstanding, envy, malice, and the desire to see the world be only what you or your tribe wanted it to be—especially when we are all enmeshed in a world where government has done so much for so long that it takes a powerful imagination to see how the human world could thrive with it doing far less—make it a long, difficult, perhaps even eternal pushback against the depredations of power. But they have provided a rich set of ideas and analysis and inspiration to help generations, both here and to come, promote and get closer to the creation of a world that respects individual liberty and property as a path to wealth and peace.

Notes

Introduction

1. Ronald Bailey and Marian Tupy, *Ten Global Trends Every Smart Person Should Know: And Many Others You Will Find Interesting* (Washington: Cato Institute, 2020): gross domestic product, p. 7; global life expectancy, p. 55; infant mortality, p. 61; battlefield deaths, p. 85; undernourished, p. 127; cereal yields, p. 132; income on necessities, p. 161.

2. Marian L. Tupy and Ronald Bailey, "More Land for Nature," Human Progress, March 1, 2023.

3. Marian L. Tupy and Ronald Bailey, "Are We Running Out of Resources?," Human Progress, March 4, 2023; Bailey and Tupy, *Ten Global Trends*, p. 11.

Chapter 1

4. Quoted in Herbert J. Muller, *Freedom in the Ancient World*, paperback ed. (New York: Bantam, 1961), p. 121.

5. Étienne de la Boétie, *The Politics of Obedience: The Discourse of Voluntary Servitude* (self-pub., 1577; repr., Auburn, AL: Ludwig von Mises Institute, 2015).

6. Herbert Spencer, "The Right to Ignore the State," in *Social Statics* (New York: Robert Schalkenbach Foundation, 1970), p. 185.

7. *Lochner v. New York*, 198 U.S. 45 (1905).

8. Quoted in W. H. Greenleaf, *The British Political Tradition*, vol. 2, *The Ideological Heritage* (London: Methuen, 1983), p. 48.

Chapter 2

9. Stephen Kresge, "Introduction," in F. A. Hayek, *Hayek on Hayek: An Autobiographical Dialogue*, ed. Stephen Kresge and Leif Wenar (Chicago: University of Chicago Press, 1994), p. 6.

10. Eamonn Butler, *Ludwig von Mises: Fountainhead of the Modern Microeconomics Revolution* (Brookfield, VT: Gower, 1988), p. 7.

11. Butler, *Mises*, p. 9.

12. For details on Mises's military service in World War I, see Jörg Guido Hülsmann, *Mises: The Last Knight of Liberalism* (Auburn, AL: Ludwig von Mises Institute, 2007), pp. 74, 258–67, 280–86.

13. Ludwig von Mises, *Socialism: An Economic and Sociological Analysis* (1922; Indianapolis: Liberty Classics, 1981).

14. Hayek, *Hayek on Hayek*, pp. 67–69.

15. F. A. Hayek, *The Fortunes of Liberalism: Essays on Austrian Economics and the Ideal of Freedom*, ed. Peter G. Klein (Chicago: University of Chicago Press, 1992), p. 133.

16. Quoted in Alan Ebenstein, *Friedrich Hayek: A Biography* (New York: Palgrave, 2001), p. 90.

17. Robert Heilbroner, "After Communism," *New Yorker*, September 10, 1990, p. 92.

18. Ludwig von Mises, *Liberalism in the Classical Tradition*, 3rd ed. (1962; Irvington-on-Hudson, NY: Foundation for Economic Education, 1985), p. 4.

19. Mises, *Liberalism*, pp. 55–56.

20. Ludwig von Mises, *Epistemological Problems of Economics* (1960; New York: New York University Press, 1981), p. 3.

21. Quoted in Margit von Mises, *My Years with Ludwig von Mises*, 2nd enl. ed. (1976; Cedar Falls, IA: Center for Futures Education, 1984), p. 58.

22. Ronald Reagan, letter to Henry Hazlitt, November 16, 1984, Henry Hazlitt Archives, Foundation for Economic Education.

23. Rose Wilder Lane, *Economic Council Review of Books*, October 1949, p. 3.

24. Henry Hazlitt, "The Case for Capitalism," *Newsweek*, September 19, 1949, p. 70.

25. Quoted in Gerald Frost, *Antony Fisher: Champion of Liberty* (London: Profile, 2002), p. 107.

26. Hayek, *Hayek on Hayek*, p. 47.

27. Hayek, *Hayek on Hayek*, p. 69.

28. Norman Barry, *Hayek's Social and Economic Philosophy* (London: Macmillan, 1979), p. vii.

29. Hayek, *Hayek on Hayek*, pp. 76–77.

30. F. A. Hayek, "Symposium on Keynes: Why?," in *Contra Keynes and Cambridge: Essays, Correspondence*, ed. Bruce Caldwell (Chicago: University of Chicago Press, 1995), p. 238.

31. F. A. Hayek, *The Road to Serfdom* (London: Routledge, 1944).

32. Albert N. Greco, *The Marketing of World War II in the US, 1939–1946: A Business History of the US Government and the Media and Entertainment Industries* (New York: Palgrave Pivot, 2020), p. 51.

33. Quoted in Caldwell, *Contra Keynes*, p. 31.

Chapter 3

34. John Chamberlain, *A Life with the Printed Word* (Chicago: Regnery Gateway, 1982), p. 136.

35. Stephen Cox, *The Woman and the Dynamo: Isabel Paterson and the Idea of America* (New Brunswick, NJ: Transaction, 2004), pp. 15–16.

36. For details on her strange relationship with her husband, see Cox, *Woman and the Dynamo*, pp. 28–31.

37. Quoted in Cox, *Woman and the Dynamo*, p. 176.

38. Cox, *Woman and the Dynamo*, p. 263.

39. Isabel Paterson, *The God of the Machine* (1943; New Brunswick, NJ: Transaction, 1993), p. 140.

40. Paterson, *God of the Machine*, pp. 12–13.

41. Paterson, *God of the Machine*, p. 196.

42. Paterson, *God of the Machine*, p. 241 (emphasis in original).

43. Paterson, *God of the Machine*, p. 66.

44. Paterson, *God of the Machine*, p. 250 (emphasis in original).

45. Quoted in Cox, *Woman and the Dynamo*, p. 287.

46. Rose Wilder Lane, *Economic Council Review of Books*, February 1946, p. 2.

47. Quoted in Cox, *Woman and the Dynamo*, p. 289.

48. Michael S. Berliner, ed., *The Letters of Ayn Rand* (New York: Dutton, 1995), p. 215 (emphasis in original).

49. Stephen Cox, "Introduction," in Paterson, *God of the Machine*, p. xxix.

50. For details on Lane's marriage and divorce, see William V. Holtz, *The Ghost in the Little House: A Life of Rose Wilder Lane* (Columbia, MO: University of Missouri Press, 1993), pp. 50–59, 71.

51. William Holtz, "The Ghost in the Little House Books," *Liberty*, March 1992, p. 54.

52. Quoted in Holtz, *Ghost in the Little House,* p. 261.

53. Rose Wilder Lane, "Credo," *Saturday Evening Post*, March 1936.

54. Jim Powell, "Rose Wilder Lane, Isabel Paterson, and Ayn Rand: Three Women Who Inspired the Modern Libertarian Movement," *The Freeman*, May 1996, p. 324.

55. Paterson, *God of the Machine*, pp. 125–26; Rose Wilder Lane, *The Discovery of Freedom: Man's Struggle against Authority* (1943; New York: Laissez Faire, 1984), pp. xi–xii (emphasis in original).

56. William Holtz, "The Woman vs. the State," *Liberty*, March 1991, pp. 46–47.

57. William Holtz, ed., *Dorothy Thompson and Rose Wilder Lane: Forty Years of Friendship, Letters 1921–1960* (Columbia, MO: University of Missouri Press, 1991), p. 195.

58. Roger Lea MacBride, ed., *The Lady and the Tycoon: The Best of Letters between Rose Wilder Lane and Jasper Crane* (Caldwell, ID: Caxton, 1973), pp. 216–17 (emphasis in original).

59. MacBride, *Lady and the Tycoon*, p. 15.

60. Lisa Duggan, "How Ayn Rand Became the Spirit of Our Time," Literary Hub, May 31, 2019.

61. Barbara Branden, *The Passion of Ayn Rand* (Garden City, NY: Doubleday, 1986), p. 60.

62. Berliner, ed., *Letters of Ayn Rand*, p. 13.

63. Berliner, *Letters of Ayn Rand*, p. 54.

64. Ayn Rand, *The Fountainhead* (New York: Bobbs-Merrill, 1943), pp. 390–91.

65. Rand, *Fountainhead*, pp. 685–86.

66. David Harriman, ed., *The Journals of Ayn Rand* (New York: Dutton, 1997), p. 86.

Chapter 4

67. Quoted in Andrew A. Workman, "Manufacturing Power: The Organizational Revival of the National Association of Manufacturers, 1941–1945," *Business History Review* 72, no. 2 (1998): 294.

68. The Conference Board, Timeline.

69. Mary Sennholz, *Leonard E. Read: Philosopher of Freedom* (Irvington-on-Hudson, NY: Foundation for Economic Education, 1993), p. 69.

70. Leonard Read, letter to James Fifield, August 9, 1945, Foundation for Economic Education Archives.

71. Leonard E. Read, *Anything That's Peaceful: The Case for the Free Market* (Irvington-on-Hudson, NY: FEE, 1964), pp. 7–8.

72. Brian Doherty, *Radicals for Capitalism: A Freewheeling History of the Modern American Libertarian Movement* (New York: PublicAffairs, 2007), p. 157.

73. Leonard Read, journal, May 22, 1958, Foundation for Economic Education Archives.

74. Leonard Read, FEE memo to the board, undated, FEE archives. Context clues indicate likely from 1953 or 1954.

75. Read, *Anything That's Peaceful*.

76. Doherty, *Radicals for Capitalism*, pp. 165–66.

77. R. C. Hoiles, *Santa Ana Register*, October 14, 1942.

Chapter 5

78. Brian Doherty, *Radicals for Capitalism: A Freewheeling History of the Modern American Libertarian Movement* (New York: PublicAffairs, 2007), p. 183.

79. F. A. Hayek, "The Intellectuals and Socialism," *University of Chicago Law Review* 16, no. 3 (1949): 417–33.

80. F. A. Hayek, *Socialism and War: Documents, Reviews,* ed. Bruce Caldwell (Chicago: University of Chicago Press, 1997), pp. 225, 227.

81. Richard Cornuelle, interview by author, September 15, 1996.

82. Cornuelle, author interview.

83. Quoted in Dyanne M. Peterson, "The Mises Centennial Celebration," *In Pursuit of Liberty*, February 1982, p. 3.

Chapter 6

84. Leonard Read, letter to Fred R. Fairchild, May 27, 1948, Foundation for Economic Education Archives.

85. R. W. Hartwell, *A History of the Mont Pelerin Society* (Indianapolis: Liberty Fund, 1995), pp. 214–15. Hayek discussed the reaction of more standard economists to Erhard's bold moves. F. A. Hayek, *The Fortunes of Liberalism: Essays on Austrian Economics and the Ideal of Freedom*, ed. Peter G. Klein (Chicago: University of Chicago Press, 1992), pp. 13–14.

86. Milton and Rose D. Friedman, *Two Lucky People: Memoirs* (Chicago: University of Chicago Press, 1998), p. 161.

Chapter 7

87. F. A. Hayek, *Hayek on Hayek: An Autobiographical Dialogue*, ed. Stephen Kresge and Leif Wenar (Chicago: University of Chicago Press, 1994), p. 126.

88. F. A. Hayek, *The Constitution of Liberty* (Chicago: University of Chicago Press, 1960), p. 6.

Chapter 8

89. Leonard Read, letter to Harvey Campbell, October 29, 1959, Foundation for Economic Education Archives.

90. Eleanor Roosevelt, "'Welfare State' Wrongly Called Communism," *Memphis Press-Scimitar*, October 31, 1951, p. 6.

91. Brian Doherty, *Radicals for Capitalism: A Freewheeling History of the Modern American Libertarian Movement* (New York: PublicAffairs, 2007), p. 196.

92. For big-picture details on the Buchanan Committee, see Brian Doherty, *Radicals for Capitalism: A Freewheeling History of the Modern American Libertarian Movement* (New York: PublicAffairs, 2007), pp. 195–97. For the quoted letter from the committee, see 96 Cong. Rec., Part 7 (June 14–July 11, 1950), pp. 9029–30.

93. William C. Mullendore, telegram to Rep. Frank Buchanan, June 5, 1950. Copy in Foundation for Economic Education Archives.

94. Frank Chodorov, *Fugitive Essays: Selected Writings of Frank Chodorov*, ed. Charles Hamilton (Indianapolis: Liberty Press, 1980), p. 63.

Chapter 9

95. Murray N. Rothbard, *The Ethics of Liberty* (1982; New York: New York University Press, 1998), p. xlvii.

96. Quoted in Justin Raimondo, *An Enemy of the State: The Life of Murray N. Rothbard* (Amherst, NY: Prometheus, 2000), p. 47.

97. Murray N. Rothbard, "What's Wrong with the *Liberty* Poll; or, How I Became a Libertarian," *Liberty*, July 1988, p. 55.

98. Murray Rothbard, letter to Richard Cornuelle, January 6, 1954, Murray Rothbard Archives, Ludwig von Mises Institute.

99. Quoted in Raimondo, *Enemy of the State*, pp. 82–83.

100. Murray Rothbard, letter to William Johnson, August 19, 1954, Rothbard Archives, Ludwig von Mises Institute.

Chapter 10

101. Milton Friedman, interview by author, January 28, 1995.

102. Milton and Rose D. Friedman, *Two Lucky People: Memoirs* (Chicago: University of Chicago Press, 1998), p. 156.

103. Friedman and Friedman, *Two Lucky People*, p. 176.

104. Friedman and Friedman, *Two Lucky People*, pp. 219–21.

105. Milton Friedman, interview by author, January 29, 1995.

106. Milton Friedman, *Capitalism and Freedom* (Chicago: University of Chicago Press, 1962), p. 2.

Chapter 11

107. Brian Doherty, *Radicals for Capitalism: A Freewheeling History of the Modern American Libertarian Movement* (New York: PublicAffairs, 2007), p. 308.

108. Benjamin Rogge, "Note on the Election," *New Individualist Review* 3, no. 4 (1965): p. 28.

109. Garry Wills, *Nixon Agonistes: The Crisis of the Self-Made Man* (Boston: Houghton Mifflin, 1970), pp. 553, 555–56.

110. Wills, *Nixon Agonistes*, pp. 555–56.

Chapter 12

111. Nathaniel Branden, *Judgment Day: My Years with Ayn Rand* (Boston: Houghton Mifflin, 1989), p. 224.

112. Nathaniel Branden, *Judgment Day*, pp. 255–56.

Chapter 15

113. Murray N. Rothbard, *Left and Right: The Prospects for Liberty* (San Francisco: Cato Institute, 1979), p. 7 (emphasis in original).

114. Murray N. Rothbard, "Confessions of a Right-Wing Liberal," *Ramparts*, June 15, 1968, p. 48.

115. Rothbard, "Confessions," p. 50.

116. Murray Rothbard, letter to W. D. Pringle, September 13, 1966, Rothbard Archives, Ludwig von Mises Institute.

117. Brian Doherty, *Radicals for Capitalism: A Freewheeling History of the Modern American Libertarian Movement* (New York: PublicAffairs, 2007), pp. 343–44.

118. For individual issues of the *Libertarian Forum*, visit the Rothbardiana website, https://rothbard.altervista.org/raccolte/the-libertarian-forum.html.

119. Donald Meinshausen, interview by author, May 15, 2004, and Meinshausen's statement submitted to the House Internal Security Committee, August 6, 1969, shared with author by Meinshausen.

120. Karl Hess, "The Death of Politics," *Playboy*, March 1969.

121. Details on the 1969 YAF convention from author interviews with attendees Karl Hess Jr., Durk Pearson, Sandy Shaw, and Don Meinshausen, and from Jerome Tuccille, *Radical Libertarianism* (1970; San Francisco: Cobden, 1985), pp. 97–109.

122. For details on SIL, see Jonathan Schoenwald, "No War, No Welfare, and No Damn Taxation: The Student Libertarian Movement, 1968–1972," in Marc Jason Gilbert, ed., *The Vietnam War on Campus: Other Voices, More Distant Dreams* (Westport, CT: Praeger, 2001); and Rebecca E. Klatch, *A Generation Divided: The New Left, the New Right, and the 1960s* (Berkeley, CA: University of California Press, 1999), pp. 234–36.

123. Klatch, *A Generation Divided*, p. 235.

124. "Anarchist Graffiti: Where Were you in '69?," *New Libertarian Notes* 2, no. 36, November 1974, p. 23.

125. Schoenwald, "No War, No Welfare, and No Damn Taxation," p. 33.

126. James Boyd, "From Far Right to Far Left—and Farther—With Karl Hess," *New York Times Magazine*, December 6, 1970.

127. Tony Lang, "Karl Hess Is Aflame with the Idea That a Man Can Run His Own Life," *Washington Post Potomac*, December 6, 1970.

128. Stan Lehr and Louis Rossetto Jr., "The New Right Credo—Libertarianism," *New York Times Magazine*, January 10, 1971.

Chapter 16

129. Murray N. Rothbard, *For a New Liberty: The Libertarian Manifesto* rev. ed. (New York: Collier, 1978); David Friedman, *The Machinery of Freedom: Guide to a Radical Capitalism* (New York: Harper Colophon, 1973).

Chapter 17

130. Milton and Rose D. Friedman, *Two Lucky People: Memoirs* (Chicago: University of Chicago Press, 1998), p. 380.

Chapter 18

131. David Nolan, interview by author, December 11, 2005.

132. Nolan, author interview; and Tonie Nathan, interview by author, December 16, 2005.

133. Bill Kauffman, "The Elector Defector," *American Enterprise*, March 2001.

134. Ed Crane, interview by author, July 7, 1998.

135. Crane, author interview.

136. Elisabeth Bumiller, "The Rich Man Out," *Washington Post*, June 19, 1980.

137. Crane, author interview.

Chapter 19

138. Robert Poole, interview by author, July 5, 1998.

139. Liberland website, https://liberland.org/en/.

Chapter 20

140. Brian Doherty and Matt Welch, "Did the Libertarian Party Blow It in 2016?," *Reason*, February 2017.

Chapter 21

141. Robert Nozick, *Anarchy, State, and Utopia* (New York: Basic Books, 1974), p. xv.

142. Julian Sanchez, "An Interview with Robert Nozick (July 26, 2001)."

143. Nozick, *Anarchy, State, and Utopia*, p. 312.

Chapter 22

144. Randy E. Barnett, *Restoring the Lost Constitution: The Presumption of Liberty* (Princeton, NJ: Princeton University Press, 2004), p. 45.

Chapter 23

145. Milton and Rose D. Friedman, *Two Lucky People: Memoirs* (Chicago: University of Chicago Press, 1998), pp. 441–59.

146. Jim Powell, "Inflation and Deflation: A Biography of Milton Friedman," July 4, 2000, Libertarianism.org.

147. Milton Friedman, "Economic Freedom, Human Freedom, Political Freedom" (speech given at California State University–East Bay, Hayward, November 1, 1991).

Chapter 24

148. Israel M. Kirzner, "The 'Austrian' Perspective on the Crisis," in *Crisis in Economic Theory*, ed. Daniel Bell and Irving Kristol (New York: Basic Books, 1981), p. 115 (emphasis in original).

Chapter 25

149. James M. Buchanan, *Better than Plowing and Other Personal Essays* (Chicago: University of Chicago Press, 1992), p. 97.

Chapter 26

150. Ronald Reagan, "Inaugural Address 1981," January 20, 1981.

151. Manuel Klausner, "Inside Ronald Reagan: A *Reason* Interview," *Reason*, July 1975, p. 6.

152. Charles Murray, interview by author, July 3, 1998.

153. Brian Doherty, *Ron Paul's Revolution: The Man and the Movement He Inspired* (New York: Broadside Books, 2012), p. 66.

154. Paul Jacob, interview by author, July 8, 1998.

155. Brian Doherty, *Radicals for Capitalism: A Freewheeling History of the Modern American Libertarian Movement* (New York: PublicAffairs, 2007), p. 454.

156. John L. Kelley, *Bringing the Market Back In: The Political Revitalization of Market Liberalism* (New York: New York University Press, 1997), p. 194.

Chapter 27

157. Quoted in David Boaz, *Libertarianism: A Primer* (New York: Free Press, 1997), p. 1.

158. E. J. Dionne, *Why Americans Hate Politics* (New York: Simon & Schuster, 1991), p. 261 (emphasis in original).

159. For a survey of post-*Kelo* reforms, see Stephen F. Broadus IV, "Ten Years after *Kelo v. City of New London* and the Not So Probable Consequences," *Mississippi College Law Review* 34, no. 2 (2015): 323–47. "While scholars and citizens were concerned that *Kelo* was a step in the wrong direction, *Kelo* led to a wave of reform which has had a positive effect on eminent domain."

160. Lane, quoted in a letter from Jasper Crane to William C. Mullendore, December 30, 1960, William Mullendore Collection, University of Oregon, Eugene, Oregon.

161. John Perry Barlow, "A Declaration of the Independence of Cyberspace," Electronic Frontier Foundation, February 8, 1996.

Index

Information in endnotes is indicated by n.

About the Author

Brian Doherty is a senior editor at *Reason* magazine. He is the author of six books, and his reporting and commentary have appeared in dozens of radio and TV programs and over 100 publications, including the *New York Times*, *Washington Post*, *Wall Street Journal*, *USA Today*, *Mother Jones*, *Wired*, and *Spin*. He won the Thomas S. Szasz Award for Outstanding Contributions to the Cause of Civil Liberties in 2011.

Libertarianism.org

Liberty. It's a simple idea and the linchpin of a complex system of values and practices: justice, prosperity, responsibility, toleration, cooperation, and peace. Many people believe that liberty is the core political value of modern civilization itself, the one that gives substance and form to all the other values of social life. They're called libertarians.

Libertarianism.org is the Cato Institute's treasury of resources about the theory and history of liberty. The book you're holding is a small part of what Libertarianism.org has to offer. In addition to hosting classic texts by historical libertarian figures and original articles from modern-day thinkers, Libertarianism.org publishes podcasts, videos, online introductory courses, and books on a variety of topics within the libertarian tradition.